# 50 GEMS

# The Lothians

JACK GILLON

AMBERLEY

# Acknowledgements

I am grateful to Alison Strauss of the Falkirk Community Trust for help with images of the Hippodrome in Bo'ness. Thanks to Michael, Tina, Oliver and Lucy for hospitality and transport during my visit to West Lothian – Michael discovered the stunning West Lothian countryside around Cairnpapple on our road trips. I also owe a debt to Daniel Lodge and Ken Tippen for help with images – Ken allowed me to use his very fine photo of Tantallon and the Bass Rock. As ever, I owe a huge thanks to Emma Jane for her continuing advice and support. It would be remiss of me to leave out the contribution of Toby Gillon, who was an enthusiastic companion on many of the visits to the sites in the book.

First published 2020

Amberley Publishing
The Hill, Stroud
Gloucestershire, GL5 4EP

www.amberley-books.com

Copyright © Jack Gillon, 2020

Map contains Ordnance Survey data © Crown copyright and database right [2020]

The right of Jack Gillon to be identified as the Author
of this work has been asserted in accordance with the
Copyrights, Designs and Patents Act 1988.

British Library Cataloguing in Publication Data.
A catalogue record for this book is available from the British Library.

ISBN 978 1 4456 9157 2 (paperback)
ISBN 978 1 4456 9158 9 (ebook)

Typesetting by Aura Technology and Software Services, India.
Printed in Great Britain.

# Contents

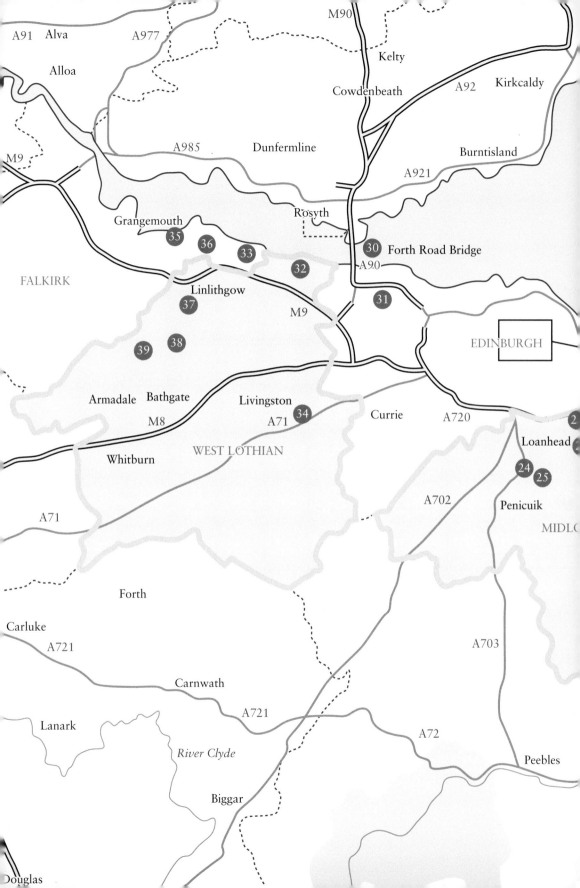

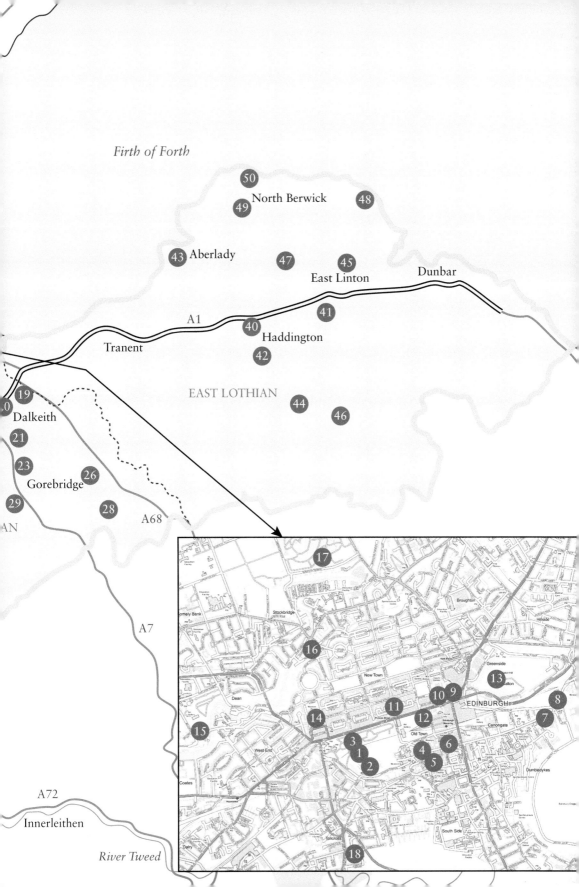

# Introduction

The Lothians consist of West Lothian (Linlithgowshire), East Lothian (Haddingtonshire) and Midlothian and Edinburgh (Edinburghshire), which nestle along the south side of the broad estuary of the Forth.

The strategic location and political and economic importance of the Lothians, with Edinburgh at its centre, have made the region witness to some of the most significant events in Scottish history. This is reflected in the remarkable wealth of architectural heritage spanning thousands of years. The Lothians have been settled since prehistoric times, as reflected in two of the gems in this book – the fortified settlement of Traprain in East Lothian and the sacred site at Cairnpapple Hill in West Lothian. Castles, royal palaces, churches and industrial buildings of national importance abound in the Lothians. *50 Gems of The Lothians* explores the places that make the Lothians special and tells the fascinating story of their rich and varied past.

With this wealth of heritage, the task of selecting fifty places to represent Lothian's rich architectural legacy has been immensely difficult and not everyone will agree with the selection. However, hopefully it will be of interest, even if your particular favourite has been omitted or you think a particular example is less than worthy of inclusion.

The historic boundaries of the Lothians, rather than the more recent local authority boundaries, are used in the book.

Please check opening times and accessibility before visiting any of the gems. An entrance charge will apply to a number of the properties and sites in the book. Many are in the care of Historic Environment Scotland.

# Edinburgh

It is the peculiar boast of Edinburgh, the circumstances on which its marvellous beauty so essentially depends, that its architecture is its landscape; that nature has done everything, has laid every foundation, and disposed of every line of its rocks and its hills, as if she had designed it for the display of architecture.

*The Edinburgh Review* (1838)

A city that possesses a boldness and grandeur of situation beyond any that I have ever seen.

Thomas Pennant, *A Tour in Scotland* (1769)

# 1. St Margaret's Chapel

Edinburgh Castle is the pre-eminent building of historic and architectural importance in Edinburgh, and Scotland's most popular tourist attraction. Dramatically situated on its precipitous crag, standing 100 metres above Princes Street, the turreted and battlemented complex of buildings towers over the city centre and dominates the skyline. It is an internationally renowned compelling architectural symbol of Edinburgh and Scotland.

The diminutive ancient Romanesque chapel, dedicated to St Margaret, stands at the highest point of the castle and is the oldest surviving building in the city.

It was built in the first half of the twelfth century during the reign of one or other of St Margaret's younger sons – David or Alexander. Queen Margaret (1045–93) was the wife of Malcolm III of Scotland – already ill, she died on hearing of the death of her husband at the Battle of Alnwick. She was canonised by Pope Innocent IV in 1250 for her charitable work and religious fidelity.

The 'Royal Chapel in the Castle' originally formed part of the royal lodgings and was used for religious services. The chapel was saved on the orders of Robert the Bruce when the castle was demolished in 1314, to prevent it from being taken by English forces.

From the sixteenth century, following the Reformation, it was used as a munitions store. In 1845, the significance of the buildings was rediscovered by the antiquarian Sir Daniel Wilson and it was partly restored in 1853.

*Above*: Edinburgh Castle from the Esplanade.

*Below*: St Margaret's Chapel.

St Margaret's Chapel, stained glass.

The striking stained-glass windows depicting St Andrew, St Columba, St Margaret and Sir William Wallace were installed in 1922. A further restoration brought the building back into use and it was dedicated on 16 March 1934. Another restoration of the building was carried out in 1993 to commemorate the 900th anniversary of the death of St Margaret.

# 2. The Scottish National War Memorial

I find it more difficult to write about Scotland's National War Shrine than about anything I have ever attempted to describe. There is nothing like it in the world: it is the soul of Scotland. I stand bereft of words in the most beautiful War Shrine in the world.

H. V. Morton, *In Search of Scotland* (1929)

*Above*: The Scottish National War Memorial.

*Left*: The Shrine, the Scottish National War Memorial.

Few families in Scotland were not touched in some way by the impact of the First World War, and the Scottish National War Memorial commemorates the sacrifices of nearly 150,000 Scots in the conflict. It was designed by Sir Robert Lorimer (1864–1929) and stands on Crown Square at the summit of the Castle Rock on the site of a barracks block that had replaced the ancient St Mary's Chapel.

A semicircular flight of steps, flanked by a heraldic lion and unicorn, leads up to the entrance porch of the memorial. The exterior gives little hint of the stunning and poignant interior, which includes a frieze carved with the names of First World War battlefields and sumptuous stained glass.

It was paid for by public subscription in Scotland and worked on by hundreds of Scottish craftsmen. The memorial was opened by the Prince of Wales on 14 July

1927. The king had made it a policy not to open any war memorials, but, shortly after the inauguration, the king, queen and Princess Mary laid wreaths outside the building and placed the rolls of honour, with the names of Scots killed in the First World War, in a casket that forms the centrepiece of the memorial.

At the time of its construction, it was believed by many that the memorial would be a shrine to the 'war that ended war', and it is sad to reflect that it now also commemorates the more than 50,000 Scots fatalities in the Second World War and conflicts since then.

# 3. The Ross Fountain

The Ross Fountain is a beautiful and intricately detailed example of nineteenth-century cast ironwork, which forms an ornamental foreground to Edinburgh Castle in West Princes Street Gardens.

The circular fountain is a riot of decoration with stylised walrus heads, mermaid figures with overflowing urns, scallop-shell basins with lions' heads, swags,

The Ross Fountain.

cornucopia, and cherub-faced spouts. Near the top are four female figures depicting Science, Art, Poetry and Industry, seated between semicircular basins. The structure is surmounted by a beautifully modelled female figure clutching a cornucopia.

The fountain was the creation of the Antoine Durenne iron foundry in Sommevoire, 150 miles south-east of Paris, France. The sculptures were by Jean-Baptiste Jules Klagmann, whose other work includes figures for the Louvre and the Medici Fountain in the Luxembourg Gardens in Paris.

A prototype of the fountain had been commissioned to appear alongside various other Durenne works for the International Exhibition held in London in 1862. One of the visitors to the exhibition was an elderly Edinburgh gunmaker and philanthropist 'with inclinations to art and natural science' named Daniel Ross. The fountain had been described as 'obtaining universal admiration' and it caught the eye of Mr Ross, who decided to purchase it for the sum of £2,000 and subsequently gift it to Edinburgh. The fountain eventually arrived at Leith in 122 pieces in September 1869.

There was much debate about its location. Mr Ross had originally requested that the fountain be placed along the upper pathway of the gardens opposite Castle Street, while there were many who preferred other prominent sites such as Charlotte Square, George Street and Lothian Road. However, opinion was severely divided on whether it should be built at all. The fountain's abundance of sculptures of bare-breasted and voluptuous ladies pouring water down their chests was considered quite shocking to a section of Edinburgh society at the time. One of the most vehemently opposed was Dean Ramsay of nearby St John's Church, who labelled the nudity-laden structure 'grossly indecent and disgusting; insulting and offensive to the moral feelings of the community and disgraceful to the city'.

The Ross Fountain's eventual site, in a secluded location under the imposing shadow of the castle, appears to be the result of a heavily debated compromise. It still didn't please everybody. As a response to the fountain's location in the then private gardens, one objector complained, 'I am sorry for the Castle, rock and the garden, and the feelings of any decent-eyed person who cannot avoid seeing this unseemly, and in its present condition nonsensical erection.'

The fountain was finally unveiled in 1872 and it was agreed that it would operate 'on a Sunday and when the band plays'. The lengthy wrangles between the city authorities and establishment concerning the fountain meant that Mr Daniel Ross did not live to see the water flowing in his generous gift.

The fountain was extensively restored in 2001 and was able to spout water for the first time in five years. However, the water was turned off again in 2008 and, after further restoration, the water flowed again in 2018.

# 4. Gladstone's Land, Lawnmarket

The population of Edinburgh gradually increased within the restrictive town walls during the seventeenth and early eighteenth centuries. Separate medieval settlements, Edinburgh and the Canongate, developed. Edinburgh contained the tallest series of

Gladstone's Land.

urban domestic buildings of their time, which contrasted with the larger houses and generous gardens of the more spacious Canongate.

Edinburgh's early multistorey buildings are typified by the seventeenth-century restored tenement of Gladstone's Land. The distinctive tall and narrow six-storey building with its arcaded ground floor (a practical arrangement providing shelter for the shop stalls), curved stone forestair and small-pane, leaded glazing over timber shutters is one of the finest and most original surviving examples of an early seventeenth-century tenement ('Land' means 'a tenement') building in the Old Town.

The original house, which dated from 1550, was purchased by Thomas Gledstanes (Glaidstanes), a wealthy merchant, on 20 December 1617. Gledstanes significantly redeveloped the original building in two stages. In 1620, the building was extended forward with a wooden frontage, providing an additional room on each floor, and, in 1631, a new ashlar frontage supported by an arcaded ground floor was added.

The dignified arcaded frontage is the only surviving example of what was once a common feature of Old Town houses. They developed from the overhanging timber galleries, which were replaced from the end of the sixteenth century by stone. There was a requirement to maintain a covered passage for pedestrians to pass along the street under cover and the new stone frontages were supported by arcades with the main ground-floor frontage set back.

Gledstanes married Bessie Cunningham on 27 August 1607 and the western skewputt is inscribed with their initials – the skewputt to the east is inscribed with a saltire. The 'Gled' in Gledstanes is derived from the old Scottish word for a hawk, and the sign above the entrance includes a gilded hawk.

In the early nineteenth century many of the wealthier Old Town residents had decamped to more salubrious houses in the New Town and properties in the Old Town, including Gladstone's Land, were neglected and spiralled into dereliction. By the 1930s, Gladstone's Land was a dilapidated slum subdivided into as many as twenty-four separate units and was programmed for demolition. In 1934, it was rescued by Miss Harrison, a philanthropic local resident, who donated it to the National Trust for Scotland. It was restored by Sir Frank Mears and leased to the Saltire Society.

In 1978, a more extensive restoration programme under the direction of Robert Hurd and Partners to convert it into a museum of Old Town life was commenced. This revealed the arcaded frontage, which had been covered by a later addition shop front. Hurd carried out further work in 1978–80, which restored the timber shop booth behind the arcade and the historic window pattern. The restoration of the interior included the removal of multiple layers of paint, which revealed a finely detailed painted frieze, ceilings and shutters that are considered among the best seventeenth-century examples in Scotland.

The authentically restored and furnished building is a popular tourist attraction offering a taste of life in seventeenth-century Edinburgh and providing a striking contrast with the Trust's Georgian House at No. 7 Charlotte Square.

# 5. St Giles (High) Kirk and The Thistle Chapel, High Street and Parliament Square

The area around Parliament Square, which was built in 1632 as the forecourt of Parliament House, is the traditional site of the three estates: the three main functions of state in Scotland – church, parliament and law.

St Giles, the High Kirk of Edinburgh, has its origins in the mid-twelfth century and has been the central feature of the Old Town for nearly 800 years. It is named after a seventh-century hermit – the patron saint of cripples, beggars, lepers and blacksmiths – and was built on an older ecclesiastical site.

It has gone through numerous changes in the course of its long history and has been added to in a piecemeal fashion. The church was rebuilt after it was burned down by Richard II in 1385 during the sacking of Edinburgh and the core of the

*Above*: St Giles.

*Right*: The construction of the Thistle Chapel.

*Above left*: Thistle Chapel

*Above right*: Carved detail of an angel playing bagpipes, Thistle Chapel.

building dates from the fourteenth century. The landmark crown spire surmounted by a gilded cockerel and supported by eight flying buttresses was added around 1495 and rebuilt in 1646.

It was converted for Presbyterian worship during the Reformation and John Knox served as minister from 7 July 1559 until his death in 1572. It was briefly an episcopal cathedral between 1633–38 and 1661–89, which was not popular with many Edinburghers. On Sunday 23 July 1637, Jenny Geddes, an Edinburgh cabbage seller, famously threw a stool at the minister (this was a time when there were no seats in churches and worshippers provided their own) who was reading from the English prayer book (the Laud's Liturgy). Jenny is said to have shouted, 'False thief, will you say mass about my lug.' The result was a riot, the National Covenant and civil war, during which many Covenanters were persecuted

The church was subdivided for the use of four different congregations in the seventeenth century – the High Church, the Old Church, the Tolbooth Church and the New North, Little or Haddo's Hole Church – and fell into a state of disrepair. In 1817, the removal of the Luckenbooths, a ramshackle group of buildings that ran parallel to the church for the full length of its north side revealed the poor condition of the building.

In 1829–33, the frontage of the church was rebuilt and given a new dressed stone façade in an over-enthusiastic restoration by William Burn. Much of its medieval character was lost at this time; fortunately, funds ran out before the work extended to the open crown steeple, which retains its medieval masonry and dominates the Old Town skyline. The internal partitions were not fully removed and a single space not created until a further restoration scheme in 1881–83.

> The weather in Edinburgh on Wednesday morning was showery, but the sun shone brilliantly when the King and Queen left Holyrood for the inauguration of the Thistle Chapel at St Giles' Cathedral. Their Majesties were accompanied by the Prince of Wales and Princess Mary and the Duke of Connaught; and on their arrival were conducted to the royal pew by Lord Pentland, the chief dignitaries of the cathedral, and the leading officers of the Order of the Thistle. After a short service in the cathedral itself, the King entered the new chapel; and the Earl of Mar and Kellie and Lord Reay were invested. The royal party then returned to Holyrood. Along the route immense crowds lined the streets and cheered loudly on the royal passage.
>
> *Croydon's Weekly Standard* (22 July 1911)

The diminutive Thistle Chapel is the outstanding feature of St Giles. Designed by Robert Lorimer (1864–1929) as an addition to the south-east of the choir and opened in 1911, it is the private chapel for the Most Ancient and Most Noble Order of the Thistle – Scotland's oldest and principal order of chivalry. The order has sixteen knights, who are personally appointed by the monarch. The exquisitely decorated interior with its elaborately detailed vaulted stone ceiling, ornately carved canopied knights' stalls, intricate wrought ironwork, and heraldic stained glass is one of the finest in Scotland.

# 6. John Knox House, High Street

The picturesque John Knox's House is a fine example of a historic merchant's house and of the earliest domestic architecture in Edinburgh. It is a conspicuous building, standing forward of the street building line with its forestair and jettied timber galleries, which are the last remaining examples in the city.

It dates mainly from the sixteenth century, incorporating an earlier fifteenth-century core, and is the earliest surviving tenement in Edinburgh. It was built by James Mosman, goldsmith to Mary Queen of Scots, and bears his initials and those of his wife, Mariota Arres. The inscription 'Lufe God abufe al and yi nyghbour as yi self' is inscribed above the entrance door and there is a carved figure of Moses above a sundial on the corner. In 1573, Mosman was executed for treason (it seems that Queen Elizabeth took exception to him pawning the crown jewels and he was hung, drawn and quartered at the Mercat Cross). It is, therefore, safe to assume that the bulk of the sixteenth-century work dates from before this.

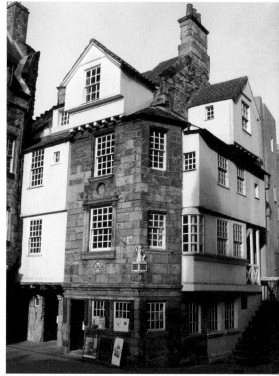

*Above left and right*: John Knox House.

The question whether the firebrand preacher John Knox ever lived in the house has been hotly contested, although there is a legend that he was resident shortly before his death on 24 November 1572 and there are stories of him preaching from the balcony of the house.

The house was in a dilapidated condition during the 1840s and in 1849 was considered for demolition for road widening. The Society of Antiquaries championed the retention of the house and its preservation had much to do with its association with Knox. The building was restored in the mid-nineteenth century, turned into a museum and has been a tourist attraction since that period. It now forms part of the Netherbow Arts Centre.

# 7. Whitehorse Close, Canongate

The Old Town is characterised by the survival of a series of tightly packed, narrow closes branching out in a fishbone pattern from the main spine of the Royal Mile – a sequence of five historic streets (Castlehill, Lawnmarket, High Street,

*Above and below*: Whitehorse Close.

Canongate and Abbey Strand). In the mid-eighteenth century there were hundreds of closes in the Old Town; there are now approximately eighty.

Whitehorse Close, at the foot of the Canongate with its idiosyncratic mix of crowstepped gables, harling walls, projecting bays, forestairs and pantiled roofs, is among the most picturesque of the Old Town closes.

The close has its origins in the early seventeenth century, when it was built with houses, stables and the White Horse Inn, on the site of the Holyrood Palace Royal Mews. The inn was the terminus of one of the first regular stagecoaches to London – a journey that took thirteen days (Scotland Yard was the London terminus for the coaches from Edinburgh). The name of the close is said to derive from a favourite horse of Mary, Queen of Scots that was stabled at the Royal Mews.

In 1745, the close was the headquarters of the Jacobite army. It was also the home of William Dick (1793-1866), who founded the city's Royal Dick Veterinary College.

In 1889, the buildings were restored and converted into fifteen houses. By the 1960s, they were much in need of repair and upgrading. In 1964–65, the extensive restoration and reconstruction work that was carried out by Frank Mears and Partners was an outstanding example of the renewal of a historically important group of buildings that had deteriorated into a slum. It is often criticised as representing over restoration and architectural fakery. However, Mears' reconstruction accentuated the historic character of the close and created what is possibly one of the most charming corners of the Royal Mile.

# 8. The Palace of Holyroodhouse and Holyrood Abbey

Legend has it that David I was knocked from his horse by a stag while hunting on a holy day. The stag then tried to kill the king, but, although wounded, he managed to grasp a cross, which miraculously appeared between the stag's antlers, at which point the animal retreated. That night St Andrew instructed the king in a dream to found the abbey in 'honour of the Holy Rood, and of St Mary the Virgin, and of all the Saints'.

The abbey was founded in 1128 and was the base of Augustinian monks who were granted the right by a charter of David I to form a new burgh between the abbey and the Netherbow – the Canongate. The Scottish kings made the abbey their main residence when they were visiting the area until James IV started to build a palace.

Between 1195 and 1230, the original abbey was rebuilt as a substantial building of great importance and splendour, consisting of a choir, transept and an aisled nave. It has been witness to some of the most dramatic moments in Scottish history. It was repeatedly burned by English armies and suffered further damage in 1559, during the Reformation. After the Reformation, the nave was used as a parish church. However, in 1570, the choir and transept were in such poor condition that they were demolished.

*Above and below*: Holyrood Abbey.

*Above and below*: The Palace of Holyroodhouse.

Holyrood Palace yard fountain.

In 1633, the abbey was remodelled for the coronation of Charles I and, in 1687, it was converted into a Roman Catholic Chapel Royal. However, in 1688, it was sacked by the Edinburgh mob following the Glorious Revolution. In 1758, a heavy stone roof was added, which collapsed on 2 December 1768, crushing the building beneath its weight and leaving the abbey as it currently stands – a roofless ruin of which only the nave remains. It is still one of the best examples of early medieval architectural work in Britain and provides an indication of how elaborate the structure must have been. It is the last resting place of a number of Scottish kings

> A house of many memories. Great people of yore, kings and queens, buffoons and grave ambassadors, played their stately farce for centuries in Holyrood. Wars have been plotted, dancing has lasted deep into the night, and murder has been done in its chambers.
>
> R. L. Stevenson, *Edinburgh: Picturesque Notes* (1879)

The Palace of Holyroodhouse developed from a royal guest house, which was part of Holyrood Abbey. It was transformed into a royal palace at the start of the sixteenth century during the reign of James IV. Additions were made between 1528 and 1536 by his son James V (1512–42), who is said to have 'built a fair palace, with three towers, in the Abbey of Hoylroodhouse'. The palace was damaged during English invasions: first by the Earl of Hertford in 1544 and again in 1650 during its occupation by Cromwell's troops.

The present palace largely dates from a reconstruction in 1671, when it was rebuilt in the French chateau style by architect Sir William Bruce (1630–1710) and builder Robert Mylne (1633–1710) for the Restoration of Charles II.

The palace is the formal Scottish residence of the Queen during state visits to Edinburgh.

The large and ornate fountain at the centre of the palace forecourt was erected as part of work to the palace grounds in the 1850s. It is a replica of the fountain at Linlithgow Palace, which dates to 1628. It was carved by John Thomas, a well-known sculptor of the time. The intricate carvings depict events from the history of the Scottish royal family and aristocratic pastimes, such as falconry and music.

# 9. General Register House, Princes Street

By the mid-eighteenth century, the need to provide accommodation for the public records of Scotland was widely recognised. Before 1662, they had been kept in Edinburgh Castle and from that date in 'two laigh rooms under the Inner Session House in a perishing condition'. A proper home for them had been proposed as early as 1722. In 1752, an Act that led to the building of the Royal Exchange gave commissioners power to build a Register House. Nothing came of these proposals until 1765, when representations to the government resulted in a grant of £12,000 being made for the construction of a 'proper repository'.

In 1767, the Earl of Morton, the Lord Clerk Register, in association with the architect, Robert Baldwin, published a design that consisted of a single-storey, square building with a central dome; however, there was disagreement over the site. In 1769, the city supplied the ground opposite the north end of the newly completed North Bridge, where a significant public building was likely to encourage the development of James Craig's design for the New Town. It was a prestigious site facing along one of the principal street vistas in Edinburgh, standing at the meeting place of the Old and New Towns and terminating the first major route between them.

In September 1769, Robert Adam, along with his brother James, received the commission for the design of the new building. Adam's design of 1771 comprised a two storey and basement building forming a rectangular quadrangle (61 metres by 47 metres) with towers projecting at each corner and halfway along each of the short sides, with the courtyard filled by a central hall under a domed rotunda surrounded by a ring of offices.

In 1773, work on the new building began. However, the scheme was reduced on financial grounds, and when the foundation stone was laid in 1774 only the south range, rotunda and the front half of the east and west ranges from the 1771 scheme were proposed for immediate construction. The structure was costly due to the need to make the building fireproof and provide stability for the storage of heavy record volumes. The money made available was insufficient, even to allow construction of Adam's reduced design. Work was suspended at the end of 1778 and the roofless shell of the building stood empty as 'the most expensive pigeon house in Europe'. In 1785, a further government grant allowed work to recommence, with the building being ready for occupation by the end of 1788.

*Above and below*: General Register House.

The building is of two storeys and on a raised basement, forming a quadrangle with a domed circular reading room. It is finished in a polished cream sandstone ashlar with projecting taller single-bay pavilions at the corners and centre of the side elevations. The towers at each end of the façade are crowned with turrets and cupolas, which project from the main wall-plane and are emphasised by Corinthian columns on their upper storeys. The ground floor and pavilions are arcaded with windows set in arches. The main south elevation has rusticated stonework at the ground floor and a Corinthian centrepiece with a pediment bearing the roundel of the royal arms. The advanced pavilions have a pair of Corinthian columns at the first floor, framing Venetian windows set in recessed arches. The interior was very simply finished except for the massive rotunda, which forms a space 21 metres high from floor to oculus and 15 metres in diameter.

Robert Adam died suddenly in 1792 before the building was complete. In 1822, it was enlarged to the dimension of Adam's 1771 design by the architect Robert Reid. In 1790, a clock was installed in the south-east tower and a weathervane in the south-west. David Bryce pushed back the front area wall in 1849, in order to accommodate the bronze equestrian statue of the Duke of Wellington.

Register House was the first purpose-built record office in Britain and is one of the oldest archive buildings still in continuous use in the world.

# 10. The Café Royal

Pubs have been the main focus of conviviality in Edinburgh for centuries and have played an indispensable part in the life of the city. It was the teeming nature of life in eighteenth-century Edinburgh that elevated the Old Town's taverns to a critical role in the city's social life and there was 'no superabundance of sobriety in the town' – in 1740, there were no fewer than 240 premises with drink licenses in the Old Town. The early Edinburgh taverns were 'in courts and closes away from the public thoroughfare and often presented narrow and stifling accommodation'. They had a 'coarse and darksome snugness which was courted by their worshippers'.

Many of these basic taverns were swept away during the period 1880–1910, which is generally recognised as the golden age of pub design. These new pubs were ornamented with an abundance of spectacular decoration to attract customers into their sparkling interiors.

The Café Royal is Edinburgh's best and most celebrated pub from this period. It is as splendid today as it was in the nineteenth century and its lavish interior reflects the heyday of the age of the most opulent Victorian pubs. Dating from 1861, it was originally built as a gas and sanitary ware showroom, became a hotel and was fitted out as a pub in 1901.

The exterior is in an exuberant French style with intricate glazing, heavily moulded console brackets, a deeply set curly pediment on the corner entrance to the Oyster Bar and a steep mansard roof, which is noted as the first of its kind in Edinburgh.

*Above*: The Café Royal.

*Below*: The Café Royal Oyster Bar.

The quality of the exterior is echoed in the lavishly decorated interior. The main Circle Bar has superb woodwork, a panelled dado, a white marble floor, a frieze decorated with ornate foliage motifs, a magnificent compartmented ceiling with hanging bosses at the intersections, a marble fireplace with an intricate over mantel, leather upholstered horseshoe seating areas and six Doulton tiled murals depicting famous inventors.

The Oyster Bar is separated from the Circle Bar by an arcaded and columned walnut screen with engraved mirror panels. The Oyster Bar retains its original red marble counter and tiled panels on the bar front. It has been described as 'one of the grandest and also the most intimate of dining rooms in Britain'. There are another three tiled murals in the Oyster Bar and eight spectacular stained-glass windows depicting British sports – bowls, tennis, archery, deerstalking, hunting, fishing, rugby and cricket.

The Café Royal came under threat in the late 1960s, when it was proposed for demolition for the expansion of a shop at the east end of Princes Street. The massive public campaign against the redevelopment of this much-cherished Edinburgh pub resulted in the building being listed in 1970 and its future secured for the enjoyment of generations to come.

# 11. Jenner's Department Store, Princes Street

Jenner's, the Harrods of Edinburgh, began life in 1838 when Charles Kennington and Charles Jenner were sacked from their jobs as Edinburgh drapers for attending the Musselburgh races rather than turn up for work. They promptly purchased the lease on a converted townhouse on the corner of Princes Street and South St David Street, and started their own drapers specialising in ladies' fashion and fancy goods. The name changed from Kennington & Jenner to Jenner's in 1868. On 26 November 1892, disaster struck when the original store burnt to the ground.

The original Kennington and Jenner shop.

*Right*: Jenner's.

*Below*: Jenner's – caryatid detail.

The new building was designed by William Hamilton Beattie based on Oxford's Bodleian Library and opened on 8 March 1895. It was one of the largest department stores in Britain when it opened and, until 2005, it was the oldest surviving independent department store in the world.

The massive six-storey building with its opulent, luxuriantly carved façade forms an impressive landmark at the corner of Princes Street and South St David Street. The splayed corner rises into an ornate richly decorated octagonal tower. The sculpted female figures (caryatids) at the first- and fifth-floor levels were intended 'to show symbolically that women are the support of the house'.

# 12. The Sir Walter Scott Monument, Princes Street

The fantastically ornate Sir Walter Scott Monument is the most prominent landmark in central Edinburgh and the largest monument to any writer in the world. Sir Walter Scott (1771–1832) was an enormously popular novelist who invented the Gothic historical novel and created the idea of Scottish Romanticism. His Waverley novels excited critical acclaim around the world. He was a prominent society figure, who rediscovered the hidden royal Scottish regalia in Edinburgh Castle and orchestrated the visit by George IV to Scotland in 1822 – the first British monarch to visit Scotland since Charles II in 1650 – for which he persuaded the king and dignitaries to wear the previously banned tartan.

The monument is made from Binny sandstone from West Lothian, designed in a Gothic style with four arched buttresses supporting a central tower. It stands just over 61 metres high with foundations that plunge around 16 metres to stand on solid rock. It took six years to build and has 287 spiral steps to the top. Within niches on the ornate façade are sixty-four character statues from Scott's novels, carved by many well-known sculptors. On the first level there is a museum room with large stained-glass panels by James Ballantine showing emblems of St Andrew and St Giles, fine decorative carved oak and gilded portrait heads of Scottish historical characters.

Following Scott's death in 1832, funds were raised by public subscription to build a suitable memorial. In 1838, a competition was arranged for the design of the monument. The final winning design was by George Meikle Kemp (1795–1844). He was a carpenter from Midlothian who had drawn Gothic architecture since his youth, was much inspired by Melrose Abbey, had been employed in the office of the Edinburgh architect William Burn and won the design competition ahead of many established architects. Kemp drowned in the Union Canal on 6 March 1844 before the monument was finished; the final works were supervised by his brother-in-law, William Bonnar.

The foundation stone was laid on 15 August 1840 and the inauguration ceremony was on the same date (Scott's birthday) in 1846. Both occasions were marked with much pomp and ceremony – processions of a mounted military band, Masonic lodges, town councillors and magistrates of Edinburgh, Canongate, Leith and Portsburgh.

*Above*: The Sir Walter Scott Monument.

*Right*: The statue of Sir Walter Scott.

Sir John Steell (1804–91) was the sculptor of the Italian Carrara double-life-sized marble statue of Scott with his deerhound, Maida, on the central platform. A bronze copy of the Scott statue was bought by expatriate Scots in America and unveiled in 1872 in New York's Central Park.

In 1997–98, a comprehensive restoration of the monument was undertaken; stone from the specially reopened Binny quarry was used to replace deteriorated masonry. The original stone, blackened by a century of smoke in 'Auld Reekie', was not cleaned as the removal of the grime would have damaged the stone.

# 13. Calton Hill and the Former Royal High School

Calton Hill includes an impressive collection of monuments. The Nelson Monument consists of a 30-metre-high circular stone signal tower, looking a lot like a telescope. The circular Dugald Stewart Monument by William Henry Playfair was erected by public subscription to commemorate Stewart (1753–1828) who was Professor of Moral Philosophy at the University of Edinburgh. The John Playfair Monument is a square, stone temple-like structure in a Greek Doric style, which commemorates John Playfair (1748–1819), Professor of Mathematics and Natural Philosophy at Edinburgh University and which was designed by his nephew W. H. Playfair.

The twelve massive columns of the unfinished National Monument on Calton Hill are known as 'Scotland's Folly' and 'Edinburgh's Disgrace', and are said to represent 'the pride and poverty of Scotland'. Although incomplete, the monument is central to Edinburgh's reputation as the 'Athens of the North'.

Calton Hill.

*Above left*: Dugald Stewart Monument.

*Above right*: The Nelson Monument.

*Right*: The National Monument.

The plan for a national monument to commemorate Scottish servicemen who died in the Napoleonic Wars was first discussed at a meeting of the Highland Society of Scotland in 1816. Supporters included Sir Walter Scott and Lord Elgin (who had removed sculpture from the Parthenon in Athens). Plans were considered for triumphal arches, and Archibald Elliot proposed a design for a circular building based on the Pantheon. However, it was finally decided that the monument should take the form of a temple structure based on the Parthenon. Charles Robert Cockerell, who was familiar with the Parthenon, was appointed architect with William Henry Playfair as his assistant. The plan was to set the building on a platform incorporating catacombs, where illustrious Scots would be laid to rest. The foundation stone was laid by George IV in 1822.

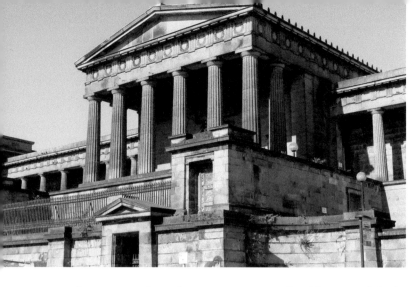

The former Royal
High School.

In 1826, work on the monument started, with some of the largest pieces of stone taken from Craigleith Quarry at Blackhall being used in its construction – twelve horses and seventy men were needed to move some of the larger stones up the hill. During the first phase of the work, over the period 1826–29, the twelve pillars cost £13,500. It was estimated that £42,000 was required for the work and, despite generous subscriptions from many eminent people including George IV, the Duke of Atholl and Sir Walter Scott, only £16,000 was raised. By 1829, funding was exhausted and the project was abandoned.

There have been many plans for the completion of the monument over the decades; however, it remains just as it did when the scaffolding came down in 1829.

The former Royal High School building occupies a spectacular location on the southern slope of Calton Hill and is recognised as a masterpiece of Greek Revival architecture. The building was designed to link in with the monuments on Calton Hill, forming a kind of Scottish Acropolis, and made a key contribution to Edinburgh's status as the Athens of the North.

The Edinburgh High School was originally founded in 1128 (making it the oldest school in Scotland) in association with Holyrood Abbey. From the sixteenth century, the school was located at the High School Yards. By the early nineteenth century, it had outgrown the High School Yards location.

In 1825, the Calton Hill site was selected for the new building. The architect was Thomas Hamilton, a former pupil of the school's predecessor. Hamilton's monumental masterwork was based on a Greek Doric temple design – the Temple of Theseus in Athens. The building consists of a central pavilion with colonnades linking on both sides to two smaller pavilions, which masterfully exploits the picturesque potential of the site.

It was not an easy location to develop and the construction involved removing a large section of Calton Hill to create a level site. The building was completed in 1829, at a final cost of £34,000 – some £14,000 over the original budget. George IV contributed £500 towards the costs and the school gained the 'Royal' appellation.

In 1968, the school moved to Barnton and the main hall in the building was converted into a debating chamber for the anticipated Scottish Assembly, prior to the 1979 devolution referendum, which failed to provide enough support for a devolved assembly. Following the Scottish devolution referendum of 1997, the proposal to use the building as the home of the Scottish Parliament was abandoned in favour of a new purpose-built building in the Old Town.

There have been various proposals for the reuse of the building; however, at the time of writing, the future use of the building is still in doubt.

# 14. Charlotte Square

Restricted for centuries by its town walls, the Old Town grew, 'piled deep and massy, close and high', and, in 1767, a beginning was made to the architect James Craig's plan for a New Town, which was intended to relieve the serious overcrowding in Edinburgh's medieval core. A complete break was made with the old city, with a new site, a gridiron plan, broad streets and formal architecture. This was followed by further planned Georgian developments up to the mid-nineteenth century which form, what have been described as, 'the most extensive example of a Romantic Classical city in the world'.

Control over the appearance of the buildings was initially very relaxed – the only condition imposed was that Craig's plan should be followed, with continuous terraces set back from the pavement by a basement area. Despite the regular plots shown on the feuing plan, feus were sold in a variety of sizes and built as both town houses and tenement blocks of different scales and designs. The development was soon criticised for its irregularity, which conflicted with the order required by contemporary taste.

In 1791, the town council commissioned Robert Adam (1728–92) to complete detailed plans and elevations for Charlotte Square. This resulted in the first New Town development to use a consistent palace block design to create an elegantly symmetrical architectural unity across a number of individual properties.

Adam died in 1792, and his original plans for parts of the square were amended following his death. However, the 100-metre-long north side of the square, which is the most elaborate, with its fine proportions and delicate detail is fully Adam's and stands as an elegant tour de force of urban architecture.

Bute House at No. 6 Charlotte Square is the official residence of the First Minister of Scotland and No. 7 is the National Trust for Scotland's Georgian House.

The north side of Charlotte Square.

# 15. Well Court, Dean Village

Dean Village, which was formerly known as the Water of Leith Village, developed at a fording point on the Water of Leith. It was already a milling community in the twelfth century and by 1700 there were several mills and two large granaries. The importance of Dean Village as a traditional crossing point of the Water of Leith ended with the completion of Telford's Dean Bridge in 1832. Before the end of the nineteenth century the water mills were redundant. In the centre of the village there is still an eighteenth-century single-arched stone bridge that once carried the old coaching route from Edinburgh to Queensferry.

In the early 1880s, the site of Well Court was occupied by some neglected tenements that were bought by Sir John Ritchie Findlay, then proprietor of the *Scotsman* newspaper. Findlay was distressed by the poverty of his less fortunate neighbours and commissioned Sidney Mitchell to design a new development of social housing on the site as a philanthropic venture – it had the additional benefit of

*Right and opposite*: Well Court.

improving the view from the rear of Findlay's house at Rothesay Terrace. In 1896, Findlay was granted the freedom of city in recognition of his philanthropy.

Well Court was built in 1883–85 and forms a quadrangle of small flats with a detached former social hall around a central courtyard. The design by Sidney Mitchell reflects the interest in traditional Scottish vernacular architecture at that period. The building is built in sandstone with red sandstone dressings and a red tile roof. The small astragalled windows, crowstep gables, turrets and flamboyant roofscape are derived from Scottish Renaissance forms and contribute to Well Court's picturesque character. The former community hall with its elaborate lead roof, gunloops and corbelled battlements is an important local landmark. The design of the five-storey clock tower is based on the seventeenth-century Earl's Palace in Kirkwall.

In 2007, Edinburgh World Heritage and the owners of the building funded a major restoration of Well Court.

# 16. St Bernard's Well

According to tradition, St Bernard's Well was rediscovered by three Heriot's schoolboys while fishing in the Water of Leith, in 1760. It takes its name from St Bernard of Clairvaux, founder of the Order of Cistercians. Legend has it that it was originally discovered by the saint in the twelfth century.

In September 1760, the mineral spring was covered by a small wellhouse. 'Claudero' (James Wilson), the contemporary poet, composed a eulogy for the occasion: 'This water so healthful near Edinburgh doth rise which not only Bath but

Moffat outvies. It cleans the intestines and an appetite gives, while morbfic matters it quite away drives.'

Chemical analysis revealed that the water was similar to the sulphur springs at Harrogate in Yorkshire. The mineral well soon became a popular resort for those afflicted by the fad for 'taking the waters'. By 1764, the well was so great an attraction that accommodation in the Stockbridge area was at a premium during the summer season. The well then resembled a Continental café with 'little tables where regulars chatted with friends'. It seems that habitual drinkers of the waters must have had cast-iron constitutions, for one later visitor likened the flavour of the water to 'the washings of foul gun barrels'.

In August 1788, the well was bought by Lord Gardenstone, who claimed he had derived great benefit from drinking the waters and, in 1789, the present construction, a circular Roman temple was commissioned by him from the architect Alexander Naismith. The elegant architectural structure, in the form of a Doric rotunda, is inspired by the Temple of Vesta at Tivoli in Italy and encloses a marble statue of Hygieia, goddess of health.

In 1885, the well and grounds were purchased by the publishers Thomas Nelson & Sons. After restoration, it was left to the city of Edinburgh. The pump room was refurbished in lavish Victorian style. The interior was designed like 'a celestial vault sparkling with sequin-like stars when sunlight strikes through the stained glass windows'. The white marble pedestal is inscribed '*Bibendo Valebis*' (By Drinking You Will Be Well).

Remarkable claims continued to be made for the well's medicinal properties, ranging from the value of a regular morning glass as a tonic for the system to a complete cure all for rheumatism and arthritis. Aerated water from the well was even bottled and marketed for a short while. The well remained popular until its closure in 1940.

# 17. The Temperate Palm House, Royal Botanic Garden

The Royal Botanic Garden began as a Physic Garden growing medicinal plants on a small site near Holyrood Palace, in 1670. By 1676, it occupied an area where the north-east corner of Waverley station now stands and was known as the Town Garden. The garden received a royal warrant as early as 1699, and in 1763 moved again to Leith Walk in the grounds of what was the old Trinity Hospital. Constantly outgrowing its various locations, it finally moved to a new site on the east side of Inverleith House, between 1823 and 1824. In 1877, Inverleith House and its policies were added to the Botanic Garden site – the extension was opened in 1881. A wealth of plant material brought back by collectors established the Botanic Garden as a major centre for taxonomic research.

The Temperate Palm House at the Royal Botanic Garden dates from 1858 and was designed by Robert Matheson. With its giant round-headed windows, Doric pilasters, slender cast-iron columns and a soaring iron and convex glass dome, it is a stunning example of Victorian architecture and engineering. At an imposing 22 metres in height, it is the tallest glasshouse in Britain. The Palm House was built at the peak of the Victorian mania for the collection of exotic plants and Parliament provided a grant of £6,000 for the construction of the building.

The Temperate Palm House.

# 18. The King's Theatre

The King's Theatre, 'the Grand Old Lady of Leven Street', is one of Scotland's most historic theatre venues. Two different architects were responsible for the design of the King's – James Davidson and J. D. Swanston. Davidson, a Coatbridge-based architect, took charge of the graceful symmetrical Edwardian baroque red-sandstone exterior of the building, with its neat double windows and ornate projecting central bay over the entrance. The façade reflects Davidson's experience in the design of solid civic buildings. J. D. Swanston, a Kirkcaldy-based architect with experience of theatre design, was responsible for the flamboyant interior, which contrasts with the rather stern frontage.

The King's first opened on 8 December 1906 with a festive production of the pantomime *Cinderella* – the annual pantomime tradition at the theatre has continued ever since. It was reported that tickets were at a premium for the opening night and a large group of spectators had to be controlled by police outside the theatre, which was brightly lit and decorated with hanging baskets. The interior 'charmed the eye with the artistic harmony of the decorations in rose and white and gold which alike under brilliant light and partial shadow present an elegant appearance'.

Over the decades, the King's has played host to some of the greatest national and international performers and companies, and the biggest stars of opera, dance, variety, screen and stage.

The King's Theatre.

# Midlothian

Midlothian is the first in political importance; from which strangers who mean to visit the most remarkable scenes in our native land set out on their various excursions, and which, independent of these circumstances, would be well entitled to the precedence, from the general fertility of its soil, the rich variety of prospect which it everywhere presents, and the internal treasures with which it abounds.

*The Traveller's Guide Through Scotland* (1814)

# 19. Dalkeith House

This is the residence of the Duke of Buccleugh, and stands about six miles from the city of Edinburgh, on the southern bank of the North Esk, and in the immediate neighbourhood of Dalkeith. It is erected on the site of an old castle, which was long the property of the family of Douglas. The Regent Morton frequently dwelt in this castle during the time that James VI was a minor. The present house was erected about the close of the seventeenth century. It consists of a main body and two wings, having some ornaments in front of it of the Corinthian order.

*A New Guide to Edinburgh* (1825)

Dalkeith House has its origins in the twelfth century as a small castle, strategically located above a meander in the River North Esk. Originally in the ownership of the Graham family, the estate passed to the Douglas family in the early fourteenth century. In the mid-fifteenth century, James Douglas became the Earl of Morton and, from 1574, Regent Morton extended the castle. In 1642, the estate was sold by the Douglas family to Francis Scott, 2nd Earl of Buccleuch. Between 1701 and 1711, the Buccleuch family commissioned the architect James Smith to create a new fashionable classical mansion based on the Palace of Het Loo in the Netherlands.

The remodelled Dalkeith House was described as 'the grandest of all early classical houses in Scotland', and its status made it popular with important visitors to the area – Bonnie Prince Charlie in 1745, George IV in 1822 and Queen Victoria in 1842.

*Above*: Dalkeith House.

*Below*: The Montagu Bridge.

The Duke of Buccleuch still maintains ownership of Dalkeith Palace; however, it has not been lived in by the Buccleuch family since 1914. Polish troops were billeted in the building during the Second World War, the house was used as the offices of a computer firm in the 1970s and early 1980s, and since 1985 it has been leased to the University of Wisconsin as its Scottish base.

The lofty single-span semicircular arch of the Montagu Bridge over the North Esk dates from 1772 and was designed by the eminent architect Robert Adam. It is considered to be a particularly outstanding example of eighteenth-century engineering. The bridge is named for Lady Elizabeth Montagu, the wife of Henry, 3rd Duke of Buccleuch.

# 20. The Collegiate Church of St Nicholas Buccleuch, Dalkeith

The imposing St Nicholas Buccleuch Church at the east end of Dalkeith High Street incorporates important examples of late medieval architecture. A chapel dedicated to St Nicholas was probably in existence on this site by the late fourteenth century. In 1406, it became a Collegiate Church and was endowed by Sir James Douglas, 1st Earl of Morton – a monument to Douglas and his wife Princess Joanna, daughter of James I, is included within the building.

In 1592, the church became the Presbyterian Parish Kirk, around which time the chancel was abandoned and remains in a ruinous condition. By the mid-nineteenth

*Above and overleaf above*: The Collegiate Church of St Nicholas Buccleuch.

century, the church was in need of substantial repairs and the architect David Bryce took control of the restoration between 1851 and 1854 – the original walls of the fifteenth-century church were incorporated in the new building. In 1885, a fire destroyed the steeple, which was rebuilt in 1888. The graveyard contains a good selection of eighteenth- and nineteenth-century monuments. A watch-house, dating from 1827, is also incorporated in the boundary wall – this would have been used for watching over graves for a suitable period after an internment, during the time when grave-robbers were prevalent.

# 21. Newbattle Abbey

Newbattle Abbey is situated on the spot formerly occupied by the abbey of Newbattle, which was founded here for a community of Cistercian monks, by King David I. The house contains many fine paintings, and is surrounded by a verdant lawn, interspersed with some straggling trees of great size, amongst which, in the graphic words of a historian of the seventeenth century – instead of the old monks are now to be seen the deer.

Robert Chambers, *The Picture of Scotland* (1827)

Newbattle Abbey stands on the site of a Cistercian monastery, which was founded by David I in 1140. The Newbattle monks prospered from thriving commercial enterprises – high-quality wool from sheep farming, salt pans at Prestonpans and

Newbattle Abbey.

working what is thought to have been the first coal mine in Scotland. The abbey was damaged over the centuries during various incursions by English armies.

After the Dissolution of the Monasteries and the Reformation, the Newbattle estate was given to Mark Kerr, the lay Abbot of Newbattle Abbey, in 1560, when he made a timely change from Catholic to Protestant. His son was made Earl of Lothian and a grand mansion was built on the site.

The original house has been remodeled and extended by some of Scotland's most eminent architects over the centuries and is now an outstanding architectural edifice set in 225 acres of beautiful formal gardens and woodland.

In 1937, Philip Kerr, 11th Marquis of Lothian, gifted the house to the nation for use as a college of adult education. It was occupied by the army during the Second World War and reopened as a college in the 1950s.

# 22. Melville Castle

Melville Castle stands on the northern bank of the North Esk, near the village and parish church of Lasswade. The principal part of the building is of a square form, with circular towers at the angles, of elegant workmanship. Two wings, appropriately neat, but not so high, are attached to the main building. The Castle being situated rather low, does not command a very extensive prospect, nor can it be seen at any great distance. The grounds are very tastefully laid out. Melville Castle is the seat of Robert, Viscount Melville, who is at present, and has been for some time, first Lord of the Admiralty. The title was conferred on his father, the celebrated Henry Dundas, in 1802.

*The Mirror of Literature, Amusement, and Instruction* (1824)

Melville Castle.

In 1155, the Melville estate was in the ownership of Baron Galfrid de Malleville. It remained in his family until 1371, when it passed to Sir John Ross of Halkhead. Mary, Queen of Scots was a frequent visitor to the castle and her Italian secretary, David Rizzio, took rooms in the castle, which became known locally as 'Rizzio's house'.

In 1765, Henry Dundas, the 1st Viscount Melville, acquired the estate and much of his wealth through marriage to the daughter of the then owner of the castle. Dundas commissioned James Playfair, the prominent Scottish architect, to replace the twelfth-century tower house on the site with an impressive new mansion house, which was completed by 1788. Queen Victoria was a guest at the castle in 1842 and Sir Walter Scott wrote about 'Melville's Beechy Grove' in his poem 'Grey Brother'. After the Second World War, the castle was leased as an army rehabilitation centre and later as a hotel. The building was vacant and in a state of disrepair by the 1980s. It was restored during the 1990s and opened as a four-star hotel in June 2003.

# 23. Newtongrange, Lady Victoria Colliery

In the 1890s, Newtongrange, 'Nitten' as the town is known locally, became Scotland's largest mining village after the Lothian Coal Company opened the Lady Victoria Colliery. The Lady Victoria Colliery was sunk in 1890 when Schomberg Kerr, the 9th Marquis of Lothian, went into partnership with Archibald Hood (1823–1902), the Midlothian coalfield entrepreneur, as the newly formed Lothian

The Lady Victoria Colliery.

Coal Company. It takes its name from Lady Victoria Alexandrina Montagu Douglas Scott, eldest daughter of the 5th Duke of Buccleuch. The pit came into production in 1894 and was the main source of employment in Newtongrange for decades.

The shaft was the deepest in Scotland and originally employed 120 pit ponies pulling coal wagons to and from the pit base. The 85-foot-high winding tower was made by Sir William Arrol & Co. in 1893. The shortened chimney, originally 150 feet tall, provided the updraft for the steam boilers.

The colliery was nationalised in 1947 and closed in 1981. It reopened again in 1984 as the National Mining Museum Scotland and is one of the best-preserved Victorian pits in Europe. Eight collieries have operated in the area since the Second World War: Whitehill at Rosewell, Arniston at Gorebridge, Burghlee and Ramsay at Loanhead, Moat at Roslin, Lingerwood at Newtongrange, Lady Victoria at Newtongrange and Bilston Glen. All have vanished without much trace, with the exception of the Lady Victoria.

# 24. Roslin and Roslin Castle

Roslin and its adjacent scenery have associations, dear to the antiquary and historian, which may fairly entitle it to precedence over every other Scottish scene of the same kind.

Sir Walter Scott, *Provincial Antiquities of Scotland* (1826)

*Left and below*: Roslin
Castle.

Roslin is the modern spelling of the village name, but the original form is Rosslyn, which is derived from the Celtic words *ross* for a rocky promontory and *linne* for a waterfall. In the mid-fifteenth century, Roslin was the third largest town in Lothian and was granted burgh of barony status in 1456. The Battle of Roslin is marked by a cairn on the outskirts of the village. The battle, on 24 February 1303, was one of the largest in Scotland during the First Scottish War of Independence, in which a Scottish army consisting of around 8,000 men defeated Edward I's larger mounted English army of up to 30,000.

Roslin also has some claim to fame as the birthplace of John Lawson Johnston, the man that gave Bovril to the world, who was born at No. 29 Main Street, Roslin, in 1839. Johnston was a butcher with an interest in preserving, which led him to experiment with using leftover beef trimmings to make a concentrated beef extract. This sold so well that he opened a factory in the Holyrood area of Edinburgh. In 1871, he moved to Canada and set up business producing 'Johnston's Fluid Beef', which was renamed the catchier Bovril – Johnston liked the word 'Vril' (an electric fluid), which he found in a book, combined with the first two letters of the Latin word for beef, '*Bos*'. In 1880, Johnston moved to England, where he lived at 'Bovril Castle' in Sydenham. In 1896, he sold the Bovril Company for an estimated £2 million. Johnson died aboard his yacht in Cannes, France, on 24 November 1900. Some 3.5 million jars of Bovril are still sold in Britain each year.

> Roslin Castle stands on an insulated rock, in a delightful glen, on the north side of the river Esk, which gushes through a deep rocky bed, wooded down to the very edge, and in many places overhung with trees. The access to the castle is on its east side, by an arch thrown across a steep ravine, and through a gateway of extraordinary strength, of which a small vestige only now remains, scarcely adequate to convey a just idea of its original importance. Over a portion of the vaulted foundation, near the posteru, and on the east side of a spacious court, now filled with huge masses of the ruins, Sir William St Clair built a modern house in 1622, over the doorway of which is a ragged cross, the armorial of the family, with his initials, and the date of erection.
>
> Charles Mackie, *The Castles Palaces and Prisons of*
> *Mary of Scotland* (1849)

The precipitous approach bridge to the ruined gatehouse of Roslin Castle stands high above the beautiful Roslin Glen. The massive and picturesque Roslin Castle was begun in around 1330, the same year as the Battle of Roslin, and it was here that Henry St Clair, 1st Earl of Orkney and Baron of Roslin, and generations of his family lived in regal splendour.

In 1544, the castle was burned by the Earl of Hertford, during the War of the Rough Wooing, but was rebuilt for the 5th Earl (William St Clair) in 1597. In 1650, Roslin was damaged again by the artillery of General Monck, Cromwell's commander in Scotland, and again in 1688 by an anti-Catholic mob. By the eighteenth century, the castle was dilapidated and only part of the east range remained habitable. The oldest parts of the castle are now the much decayed fifteenth-century keep and adjoining buttressed wall. The eastern range, which dates to 1622, was restored in the 1980s and is now let as holiday accommodation by the Landmark Trust.

# 25. Roslin Chapel

It is a specimen of the ecclesiastical architecture of Scotland that is without peer. Outside and inside it is a truly beautiful object.

> William and Mary Howitt, *Ruined Abbeys and Castles of Great Britain* (1864)

The foundation of Roslin Chapel, known as 'the chapel amidst the woods', was laid in 1446 by William St Clair (Sinclair), Earl of Caithness and Orkney. The St Clairs of Roslin were one of the most powerful families in Scotland in the later Middle Ages. St Clair is said to have 'caused artificers to be brought from other regions and forraigne kingdomes' to work alongside skilled Scottish craftsmen on the construction of the chapel.

The chapel is famed for its profusion of elaborate and luxuriant sculptural stone carving which covers almost every part of the building's interior. It is a triumph of medieval masonry and has been described as 'one of those architectural wonders whose intricate beauties and peculiarities extort our admiration while they baffle description'. The carvings are diverse in their subject matter and are both sacred and worldly; they range from supernatural animals, intricate floral designs, to religious figures.

After the death of Sir William St Clair in 1484, his ambitious plans for the chapel were never fully realised by his son and successor, Sir Oliver St Clair, and only the choir of the church with its flying buttresses and crocketed pinnacles was completed. The chapel fell into disrepair in the latter part of the sixteenth century

Roslin Chapel.

*Above left*: Roslin Chapel, the Prentice Pillar.

*Above right*: Annie Wilson.

The former Roslin Inn.

and Cromwell's troops used the building as a stable after the Battle of Dunbar, in 1650. In 1688, it was damaged by an Edinburgh mob and was restored in 1862 by the Earl of Roslin as a private chapel for the Earls of Roslin. The vaults are the last resting place of many Barons of Roslin.

The exquisite workmanship of the celebrated Prentice (Apprentice) Pillar, one of the internal columns, is a particularly outstanding feature of the sculptural detail of Roslin Chapel. It has a fluted shaft that is covered by four bands of delicate, rich foliage designs that spiral round the column with naive animal carving at the base and a deeply carved capital.

A lintel next to the Prentice Pillar has the only written inscription in stonework at the Chapel: '*Forte est vinum, fortior est rex, fortiores sunt mulieres super omnia vincit veritas*' (Wine is strong, a king is stronger, women are stronger still but truth conquers all) – a quote from First Esdras (an ancient Greek version of the biblical Book of Ezra).

The quality of the pillar's decoration is such that it has developed a tradition all of its own. This legend relates the story of the master mason who went to Italy to study the original for the proposed design. While he was absent, his apprentice, having dreamed that he had finished the pillar, carried out the final carving work. On his return, the master mason was so enraged with envy that he killed the apprentice. This well-known legend is apocryphal, as similar stories are told about a number of other churches. The story also reflects Freemasonry initiation ceremonies based on the Masonic legend of Hiram Abiff, master-mason at King Solomon's Temple.

The building beside the chapel was an inn between around 1660 and 1866. The plaque by the door records the names of some famous visitors: Dr Samuel Johnson, James Boswell, Robert Burns, Queen Victoria, Alexander Naysmith, Sir Walter Scott, Edward VII, and Dorothy and William Wordsworth. Dorothy Wordsworth wrote, 'I never passed through a more delicious dell than the glen of Roslin', and many artists depicted the glen.

The post of guide at Roslin Chapel was traditionally assigned to the proprietor of the inn and Annie Wilson, the wife of Daniel Wilson the landlord, was the official guide at the chapel for almost fifty years in the latter part of the eighteenth century and early nineteenth century. It seems that Annie, who delivered her own homespun version of the history and architecture of the chapel in a 'monotonous voice and without pauses', was one of the main perpetrators of the Prentice Pillar story. In her dual roles as innkeeper and guide, Annie met many of the celebrities of the age who visited the chapel and partook of the hospitality at the inn. Burns was so impressed by the inn that he rewarded Annie with a couple of verses scratched on a pewter plate:

My Blessings on you sonsie wife!
I ne'er was here before;
You've gi'en us walth for horn and Knife,
Nae heart could wish for more.
Heaven keep you free from care and strife,
Til far ayont fourscore;
And while I toddle on through life,
I'll ne'er gang by your door.

The chapel now looks splendid after a multimillion-pound restoration scheme. The chapel found fame through its associations with the Knights Templar and the Holy Grail in Dan Brown's bestselling book *The Da Vinci Code* and the subsequent film, starring Tom Hanks, parts of which were filmed in Roslin in 2005. The greatly increased number of visitors is catered for by a new visitor centre.

# 26. Vogrie House

The name Vogrie is derived from the Gaelic *Bhog crioch*, meaning 'boggy boundary land' and is first recorded in 1337. The estate changed hands a number of times and was acquired by James Dewar in 1719. The Dewar family were the owners of Vogrie for over 200 years. There is some debate about whether the Dewars were from the Perth whisky distilling family or from Heriot, where there was a place called Dewar or from nearby Dewarton. The family's continuing wealth was based on the ownership of local coal mines.

The estate was laid out in its present form in the early nineteenth century and the existing fine baronial-style house followed later, in 1876. The last of the Dewars at Vogrie, James Cumming Dewar, died in 1908 and his widow sold the house and estate in the 1920s to the Royal Edinburgh Hospital for Nervous Disorders for use as a nursing home. In the 1950s, it was sold to Midlothian Civil Defence and was used as a control centre for communications during the Cold War. The estate was opened as a country park in 1980. Its attractions include woodland walks by the River Tyne, an adventure play area, a nine-hole golf course and an excellent miniature railway.

Vogrie House.

# 27. Dalhousie Castle

This is a building of very great antiquity, delightfully situated on the north bank of the South Esk, a river which passes by it at only a few yards distance from the walls. It received a more modern aspect from the proprietor, the late Earl of Dalhousie, by which it has lost a considerable part of its former venerable appearance. Sir Alexander Ramsay of Dalhousie flourished in the fourteenth century, and was one of the bravest warriors of which that age could boast, under whose tuition the Scottish youth were anxious to learn the art of war.

*A New Guide to Edinburgh* (1825)

The 'stately castellated pile' of Dalhousie Castle lies to the south-east of Bonnyrigg on a meander of the River South Esk. Simon de Ramsey, an English knight, was granted Dalwolsie (the original spelling, meaning 'vale of wool') in the early twelfth century by David I of Scotland. The castle initially consisted of a fortified tower and curtain wall surrounded by a dry moat. The oldest part of the current structure dates to the mid-fifteenth century and it has been the subject of significant alteration over the centuries – its present appearance is due to the restoration and repair work in 1825 by William Burn, one of Scotland's premier architects. Edward I stayed at the castle before the Battle of Falkirk, English forces led by Henry IV besieged the castle for six months in 1400 and it was Oliver Cromwell's base during his invasion of Scotland. Dalhousie was used as a boarding school from 1927 to 1950, and in 1972 it was converted into a hotel.

Dalhousie Castle.

# 28. Crichton Castle

Crichton Castle is a fine ruin and has recently derived illustration from the pen of Mr Scott, who, in his celebrated poem of *Marmion,* has made it the scene of some striking adventures. The older part of the building is a narrow keep, or tower, such as formed the mansion of a lesser Scottish Baron; but so many additions have been made to it, that there is now a large court-yard, surrounded by buildings of different ages. All the stones on the east-front of the court are cut into diamond facets, the angular projections of which have an uncommonly rich appearance. The castle is now the property of Sir John Callender, Bart. It were to be wished the proprietor would take some pains to preserve these splendid remains of antiquity, which are at present used as a fold for sheep and wintering cattle; although perhaps there are very few ruins in Scotland which display so well the style and beauty of ancient architecture.

*Scots Magazine* (August 1808)

Crichton Castle, to the south of Pathhead, sits on raised terrace on the edge of a sharp drop to the River Tyne. Its bulk and stark outline stands in sharp contrast to the surrounding gently rolling hills.

Crichton Castle.

*Above*: Crichton Castle, the ornamental courtyard façade.

*Below*: Crichton Castle, the stables.

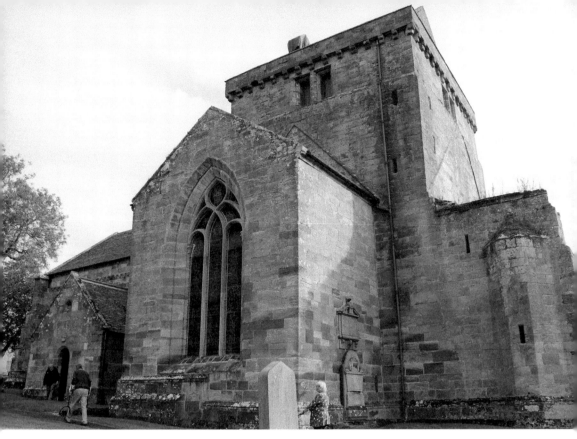

Crichton Kirk.

Although it appears consistent in appearance, it was built in a number of stages over the centuries. The oldest part is the late fourteenth-century tower house, a gatehouse was added in the early fifteenth century, a great hall in the mid-fifteenth century and further additions were made to create a fine large courtyard castle.

The outstanding feature of Crichton Castle is the ornamental courtyard façade of the north wing with its remarkable diamond-faceted masonry, which is unique in Scotland. The work was part of the Italian Renaissance additions carried out during the 1581–91 modernisation of the castle into a Renaissance palace by the 5th Earl of Bothwell, Francis Stewart, who had travelled widely in Europe. It forms an unambiguous contrast with the austere exterior of the castle.

The stable block with its distinctive horseshoe-shaped entrance arch on the south side of the castle, which was part of the sixteenth-century improvement work, is all that remains of the ancillary buildings at Crichton.

The castle stands close to the peaceful little hamlet of Crichton. Crichton Parish Kirk, the former Collegiate Church of St Mary and St Kentigren, dates from 1449 and was associated with a college established by Sir William Crichton, Lord Chancellor to James II. In 1641, it became the parish church for the area. Due to a dwindling congregation it is no longer used for regular services.

# 29. Arniston House

Arniston House is a magnificent example of a country house set in beautiful parkland. The Arniston estate lands were a royal hunting park in the Middle Ages, and were later owned by the Knights Templar. In 1571, the estate was purchased from the Crown by the Dundas family. Robert Dundas (1685–1753) was Solicitor General for Scotland, Lord Advocate and a Member of Parliament. In 1726, he commissioned the architect William Adam to design a new house at Arniston over the foundations of the original seventeenth-century tower house. Dundas ran out of money during the building works, which were completed after 1753 by William Adam's son, John Adam (1721–92).

Arniston House.

# West Lothian

West Lothian is one of the richest counties in Scotland; it is finely diversified by hill and dale, by gentle swells and fertile plains. The number of gentlemen's seats, surrounded with woods, and adorned with extensive plantations, give it a very pleasant and rich appearance. The whole is a composition of all that is great and beautiful; towns, villages and ancient towers decorate each bank of the fine expanse of water, the Firth of Forth.

*The Traveller's Guide Through Scotland* (1814)

# 30. The Forth Bridge

The opening of the Forth Bridge was celebrated yesterday with much *éclat*. Overnight the Edinburgh hotels were filled with guests who had come from all parts of Britain to take part in the ceremony. Several special trains were run to South Queensferry, and the east end of Princes Street was crowded with coaches. The route along the Queensferry road resembled the road to Epsom on Derby Day. All manner of vehicles made their way westwards, and char-a-bancs could be counted in scores. The spectacle from the bridge was most imposing. The sky was grey and forbidding, but the brightness of the steamers down below, and the exhilaration and excitement of the whole proceedings made every one careless of the elements.

*Dundee Advertiser* (5 March 1890)

The Forth Bridge flings its three double steel cantilevers across the water to the Kingdom of Fife. It is the most familiar bridge in the world. To see the Forth Bridge is rather like meeting a popular actress, but with this difference: it exceeds expectations. It is a memorable sight.

H. V. Morton, *In Search of Scotland* (1929)

The Forth Bridge was inaugurated amid much ceremony by Albert Edward, Prince of Wales on 4 March 1890 by the insertion of a gold-plated rivet in the bridge. A rail bridge across the Forth, linking Lothian and Fife, was first proposed in 1818,

*Above*: The Forth Bridge.

*Left*: View from atop the Forth Bridge.

The Ferry.

although a tunnel was considered by some as a better option. The Forth Bridge Company, which was founded in 1873, appointed Thomas Bouch as the engineer in charge of the contract. However, after Bouch's Tay Bridge collapsed in high winds on 28 December 1879, Bouch's scheme was abandoned – a brick pier from the Bouch design remains near Inchgarvie rock.

Two railway engineers, John Fowler and Benjamin Baker, were awarded the contract for a new design for the bridge. Their proposal was for the world's earliest multi-span cantilever bridge. Work started in 1883 and it took seven years to complete, with up to 4,600 workers employed on the construction. When it was completed, it had the longest bridge span in the world and was the largest steel structure ever built. It ranked as one of the outstanding engineering achievements of the nineteenth century.

> A few figures in connection with the construction of the Bridge. Its extreme length, including the approach viaduct, is 2765 yards, one and a fifth of a mile. The weight of steel in it amounts to 51,000 tons, and the extreme height on the steel structure above mean water level is over 370 feet, while the rail level above high water is 156½ feet. About eight millions of rivets have been used in the Bridge, 748,670 cubic feet of granite, 64,000 cubic yards of concrete, and forty-two miles of bent plates used in the tubes – about the distance from Edinburgh to Glasgow. These figures will give you some idea of the magnitude of the work. It has probably cost more labour of hand and brain than was ever before expended on any structure. The works were commenced in April 1883, and it is highly to the credit of every one engaged in the operation that a structure so stupendous and so exceptional in its character should have been completed in seven years.
>
> *Dundee Advertiser* (5 March 1890)

The bridge still ranks as a masterpiece of engineering and an iconic symbol of Scotland. It was inscribed on UNESCO's list of World Heritage Sites in 2015. This recognises sites of outstanding universal value. The inscription noted that the bridge is 'a masterpiece of creative genius' and 'an extraordinary and impressive milestone in the evolution of bridge design and construction'.

In recent years the bridge was given a coating of a new paint, which is expected to last for decades – the task of painting the bridge is no longer a never-ending task.

In 2012, a bronze memorial to the seventy-three men who died building the Forth Rail Bridge and to celebrate all the people that have worked on the dangerous job of maintaining it was unveiled. The monument is engraved with the words: 'To the Briggers, past and present, who built, restored and continue to maintain this iconic structure.'

> I waited for the iniquitous ferry which crosses the Forth where a traffic bridge should be.
>
> H. V. Morton, *In Search of Scotland* (1929)

There had been a ferry at Queensferry since the eleventh century, when Queen Margaret established a service to transport religious pilgrims from Edinburgh to Dunfermline Abbey and St Andrews. In the 1920s and 1930s, the only vehicle crossing was a single passenger and vehicle ferry, but by 1958, due to increasing demand, there were four ferry boats operating 40,000 crossings annually, carrying 1.5 million passengers and 800,000 vehicles. In 1947, the UK government approved an Act of Parliament to oversee the implementation of a bridge to replace the ferry service. In 1955, an alternative scheme for a tunnel beneath the waters of the Forth was proposed, but was soon abandoned. The final construction plan for a road bridge was accepted in February 1958 and work began in September of that year. It was opened by Elizabeth II and the Duke of Edinburgh on 4 September 1964 and the ferry service was discontinued from that date. When it was completed the bridge was the longest suspension bridge outside the USA and the fourth longest in the world with a total span of 2,828 metres.

In 2017, the Forth Bridge and the Forth Road Bridge were joined by the elegant cable-stayed Queensferry Crossing.

# 31. Dalmeny

The picturesque village of Dalmeny is situated around 8 miles west of Edinburgh, a short distance to the south of Queensferry and, although now part of Edinburgh, was historically within the boundaries of West Lothian.

Dalmeny.

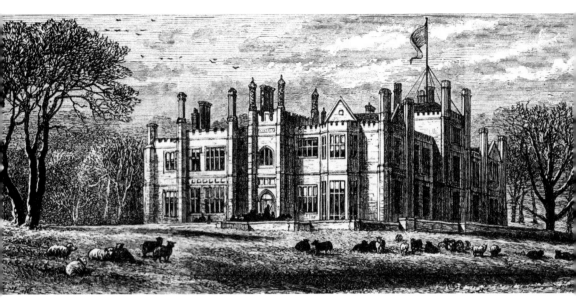

Dalmeny House.

Barnbougle.

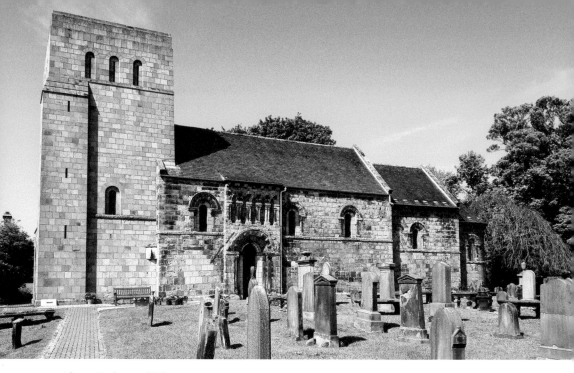

*Above*: Dalmeny Kirk.

*Below*: Dalmeny Kirk, south doorway.

The core of Dalmeny is the broad village green, the size and openness of which contrasts with the diminutive character of the stone-built cottages, with which it is surrounded.

Dalmeny is first recorded in AD 1214 and has always been primarily an agricultural village with a rural character. In the latter part of the nineteenth century, shale mines were developed in the area and a brief period of industrial activity ensued with miners' cottages, which were demolished in the 1930s, built to accommodate the population increase.

Dalmeny, as it stands today, was developed in the early 1800s by Archibald Primrose, 4th Earl of Roseberry, as a model village for Dalmeny House. Dalmeny House is a Tudor Gothic country house, which dates from 1817 and is particularly significant for its magnificent Coade stone detailing. Dalmeny House replaced the Roseberry's former residence of Barnbougle Castle on the shores of the Firth of Forth – it seems that the family resolved to decamp from Barnbougle when they were disturbed at supper by a wave breaking through the window of the dining room.

The village is dominated by the twelfth-century St Cuthbert's Parish Church, which is the best preserved Norman church in Scotland and a stunning example of Romanesque architecture. The south doorway, with its abundance of rich carvings, is a particular highlight. The west tower was built in 1937 to replace one that fell in the fifteenth century.

# 32. Hopetoun House

Here stands Hopetoun House, the princely seat of the family of Hopetoun, which never fails to delight the stranger by its external grandeur, its paintings, its charming walks and fine prospects. It is thought to be the second or third, in point of elegance of architecture, in the island. It was begun by the celebrated architect Sir W Bruce, and was finished by Mr Adam, who planned the two wings. The situation contributes much to give it that noble appearance; it has the advantage of a fine lawn in front, while at the same time it is so elevated, as to command a view of the shipping in Leith Roads, the whole Forth to North Berwick and the Bass, with the coast of Fife, bestudded with its numberless towns and villages.

*The Traveller's Guide Through Scotland* (1814)

Hopetoun House, seat of the Marquess of Linlithgow, is the focal point of magnificent designed policies and is one of the supreme palatial country houses of Scotland. There are probably few more handsome or striking residential buildings in the country. It is known as the 'the Scottish Versailles' due to the style and grandeur of the house, gardens, parkland, water features, views and woodland.

The house is associated with the Hope family. Sir John Hope (1632–82) arrived in the area in 1657 to supervise his silver and lead mining ventures. In 1696, Sir William Bruce (c. 1630–1710) was appointed to create a new country house at

*Above and below*: Hopetoun House.

Hopetoun to replace the sixteenth-century Midhope Castle, which the Hopes had acquired in 1678.

Bruce's plan consisted of a fairly modest three-storey square block. It was substantially remodelled and enlarged on a grand scale by William Adam from 1721 until his death in 1748. Robert and John Adam, William's sons, were then involved in the completion of the work, including the interior and the addition of the massive outer-wings and flanking colonnades, which make up the panoramic façade.

In 1974, the Hopetoun House Preservation Trust was created to preserve the house and estate.

# 33. Blackness Castle

Blackness Castle is dramatically located on a prominent rocky outcrop on the southern shore of the Forth – its distinctive boat-like outline has resulted in it being known as 'the ship that never sailed'.

Blackness had significant roles in the history of Scotland and was witness to many important events. The castle was inaugurated in the 1440s by Sir George Crichton, Earl of Caithness and Sheriff of Linlithgow. In 1453, It was forfeited by the Crown and was subsequently used as a state prison for political and religious prisoners. In 1481, it was attacked by an English fleet and played a key role in the wars of the Stewart kings. In the early part of the sixteenth century, the curtain walls were raised and strengthened to turn it into one of the most formidable fortresses in Scotland. However, this did not stop Cromwell's troops inflicting damage to the castle in 1650. In 1667, it was returned to use as a prison holding mainly Covenanters and, after the Union of Scotland and England in 1707, it was garrisoned by the British army. It reverted to use as a prison for French prisoners during the Napoleonic Wars and subsequently continued to serve as a military depot.

> The castle, whose battlements for many a hundred years bristled with cannon, and through whose portal bands of armed men were wont to go and come, is now let out as bathing quarters to peacefully-disposed citizens, whose children romp round its tall, gaunt towers, its grass-grown courtyard, and its gunless batteries.
>
> S.W. Partridge & Company, *The Family Friend* (1870)

In the same year as this report on the more recreational use of the castle, it was converted into an ammunition depot, with a new barracks, drawbridge and jetty added. In 1912, Blackness was handed over to the State, but was requisitioned by the military during the First World War. A major restoration programme of the castle was undertaken between 1926 and 1935.

Blackness Castle.

# 34. Jupiter Artland

Bonnington House, near Wilkieston, is an impressive Jacobean-style mansion dating from 1858, with an original house of 1622 at its core. In 2009, the extensive grounds were transformed into a contemporary outdoor sculpture park hosting exceptional

*Left*: Jupiter Artland, *Love Bomb*. (Marc Quinn)

*Below*: Jupiter Artland, *Cells of Life*. (Charles Jencks)

installations by prominent artists. The largest, and possibly most striking, is the giant sculpted grassy dunes by Charles Jencks, which flank the driveway to the house. The woodland walk is garlanded with works by artists of the status of Andy Goldsworthy and Ian Hamilton Finlay. Jupiter Artland is a unique way to experience great works of art in a stunning environment.

# 35. The Bo'ness and Kinneil Railway

After the demise of steam-powered locomotives in 1968 there was an extensive interest in their preservation. In 1979, The Bo'ness and Kinneil Railway was established by the Scottish Railway Preservation Society, with the aim of safeguarding the legacy of steam. The tireless hard work of an enthusiastic band of volunteers over the decades has transformed the initial aim of preservation into a major attraction for anyone with even a passing interest in railway heritage.

The station at Bo'ness was built on a site previously occupied by railway sidings and other industrial uses. The buildings, which have been constructed or salvaged and re-erected from other locations, reflect the heyday of steam. There are three stops on the line at Kinneil, Birkhill and Manuel.

A fine collection of locomotives, a gift shop, cafe and an extensive model railway, housed in an old railway carriage, complete the range of attractions at Bo'ness.

*Below left*: Bo'ness and Kinneil Railway poster.

*Below right*: Bo'ness and Kinneil Railway, getting up some steam.

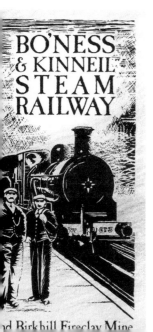

*Above*: Bo'ness and Kinneil Railway, Birkhill station.

*Below*: Bo'ness and Kinneil Railway, the model railway.

# 36. The Hippodrome, North Street, Bo'ness

The Hippodrome in Bo'ness is of particular importance as Scotland's oldest surviving purpose-built cinema.

Provost Grant performed the grand opening ceremony of the Bo'ness Hippodrome ('the Hippo') on 11 March 1912. It was a venture by a local showman, Louis Dickson, the sole proprietor and manager, and was designed in the fashionable modern movement style by local architect Matthew Steele. The opening night was billed as *Dickson's Royal Electric Pictures and Special Variety Programme*, including The Lolo May Trio of Lady Acrobats and the comedians Chorley and Connor.

The circular auditorium was multifunctional to accommodate films, variety shows and circuses. Two weeks after the opening night, on 23 March 1912, the Hippodrome hosted a mass meeting of miners and, in December 1912, Bo'ness' first pantomime, *Cinderella*. It later became a full-time cinema and was billed as Bo'ness' Super Cinema. A big attraction at the Hippodrome were films shot locally, which would draw huge audiences in the hope that they would be seen on screen.

The last film was shown in 1975 and it was used as a bingo hall until 1980 when it was disused, with dereliction following. The Scottish Historic Buildings Trust and a number of other organisations came together to restore the building and, on 9 April 2009, it reopened as a cinema.

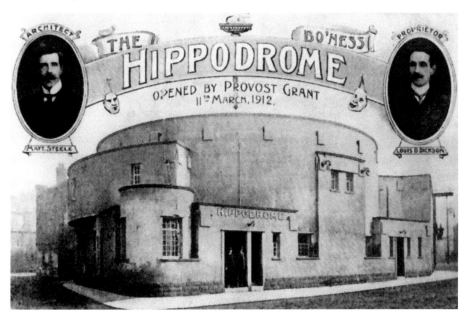

Hippodrome, postcard commemorating opening.

*Above*: The Hippodrome. (© Falkirk Community Trust)

*Left*: Inside the Hippodrome. (© Falkirk Community Trust)

# 37. Linlithgow Palace

THE spectacle of an ancient Palace, which at one time enshrined the royal honours of Scotland, and resounded alternately with the clang of arms, and the dulcet notes of peace, now left to ruin and desolation, cannot fail to inspire feelings of melancholy and regret in the bosom of the lover of the departed glories of his country. Linlithgow Palace is venerable for its antiquities, and must be ever hallowed by the many mournful recollections connected with them.

Charles Mackie, *Historical Description of the Royal Palace of Linlithgow* (1830)

Linlithgow, West Lothian's county town, takes its name from the Brythonic, Linliden, meaning 'dear broad lake', and, quite appropriately, the beautiful Linlithgow Loch is one of the principal landmarks of the town

Linlithgow Palace on the shore of the loch has a long and illustrious history. The palace was inaugurated by James I as an imposing royal residence in 1425, on the site of a thirteenth-century castle. It developed into a formal courtyard structure, with significant additions at the behest of future kings over the following centuries. Mary, Queen of Scots, was born at the palace in December 1542. The Union of the Crowns in 1603 meant that the palace ceased to be a regular royal residence.

The elaborate fountain in the courtyard at Linlithgow Palace dates from 1538. The fountain ran with wine when Bonnie Prince Charlie visited Linlithgow in 1745 – although the Duke of Cumberland's army withdrawing after Culloden destroyed most of the palace buildings in January 1746. The ruins have been kept in good order since the early nineteenth century.

The adjoining Church of St Michael was first consecrated in 1242 on the site of an earlier ecclesiastical building, although much of the present building dates from

*Above*: Linlithgow Palace and the Church of St Michael over Linlithgow Loch.

*Below*: Linlithgow Palace.

the mid-fifteenth century. It is one of the finest medieval churches in Scotland and was much favoured as a place of worship by Scottish royalty – Mary, Queen of Scots was baptised in St Michael's Church. The original stone crown tower was removed in 1821 and replaced by an aluminium version in 1964.

# 38. Cairnpapple Hill

The outstanding views from the top of Cairnpapple Hill command a wide area of central Scotland, which no doubt contributed to its sacred significance for prehistoric communities as a site of ritual and burial. It is recognised as one of the most important prehistoric sites in Scotland.

Excavation of the site in 1948 under the direction of Stuart Piggott, Professor of Prehistoric Archaeology in the University of Edinburgh, revealed that it had been first used from 3500 BC as a ceremonial site.

The earliest structure on the site is a horse-shoe group of standing stones at the base of which cremated human bones were deposited. At a later date, this was superseded by an oval shaped henge of twenty-four stones enclosed by a ditch and banking with entrances to the north and south. At the base of the stones there were signs of burials accompanied by early Bronze Age Beaker pottery vessels. The next phase involved the removal of the henge stones and the construction of a large 15-metre-diameter cairn enclosing a burial with a Bronze Age food vessel. The cairn was later enlarged to twice its original diameter. A concrete dome now replicates the outline of the solid cairn and the interior can be accessed by a ladder.

Aerial view of Cairnpapple Hill.

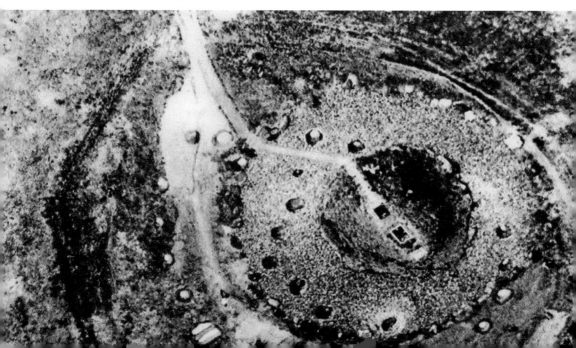

Cairnpapple Hill

# 39. Torphichen Preceptory

The Order of St John of Jerusalem was founded in Jerusalem during the First Crusade, and at the outset was preponderately a nursing brotherhood. Torphichen Preceptory was the principal residence of the Scottish Knights Hospitallers from 1153 and the chief part of the building still stands. The Order was expelled from the Holy Land as a result of the fall of the Latin Kingdom in 1291, and became established in Rhodes. From 1529 to 1798 its headquarters were on the island of Malta. In certain countries the Order was suppressed during the Reformation period, and by the year 1798 it was everywhere virtually extinguished. The Priory of Scotland was founded in 1124, but perished in the early stages of the Reformation, being dissolved in 1554. Now, after almost 400 years, it has been revived and reconstituted.

*Falkirk Herald* (2 July 1947)

Torphichen Preceptory is located in a tranquil spot to the north of the village of Torphichen. The preceptory was the major Scottish base of the Knights Hospitaller of the Order of St John of Jerusalem. The Knights Hospitaller were established during the Crusades to provide care for sick, poor or injured pilgrims visiting the Holy Land.

The order first arrived in Scotland in 1132 and was granted a charter to build a preceptory at Torphichen, on a site that had a long history of ecclesiastical use. Life in the preceptory involved running the hospital and religious devotions.

The remains of the thirteenth-century cruciform preceptory church are the north and south transepts, the crossing, the bell tower, the foundations of the cloister to the north and the choir to the east. In 1756, the nave of the preceptory was demolished and its site used for the new parish church. The remaining parts of the original

Torphichen Preceptory.

church retain fine early masonry work. Extensive restoration work was carried out on the building in 1929 by HM Office of Works.

Before the Battle of Falkirk in July 1298, William Wallace used the preceptory as a base and Edward I was treated at the hospital after the battle. The Knights Hospitaller were on the English side during the Wars of Independence and left the country after the Battle of Bannockburn in 1314, returning after an appeasement with Robert the Bruce.

# East Lothian

Taking it in general, East-Lothian may be reckoned the richest and most beautiful county in Scotland. Having nearly two sides begirt by the sea, it derives a great part of its beauty as well as opulence from this circumstance.

*The Traveller's Guide Through Scotland* (1814)

# 40. The Collegiate Church of St Mary the Virgin, Haddington

St Mary's Church in Haddington sits in a tranquil setting on the wooded banks of the Tyne. It is the largest parish church in Scotland – 63 metres long, making it slightly larger than St Giles' Cathedral in Edinburgh and similar in scale to many smaller Scottish cathedrals.

The first record of a church on the site dates from 1139. This Norman structure would have been much smaller than the existing church. It was known as 'the Lamp of Lothian'. The church was burnt twice in the thirteenth century by English armies. Again, in 1356, Edward III of England invaded Scotland and destroyed the church.

In 1380, work began on the present church and it was not completed for almost a century. The scale of the building is reflected in the period of great prosperity in Scotland, at the time of its construction. However, further destruction followed, in 1548, when the English army occupied the town during the Siege of Haddington.

Following the departure of the English army, only the nave of the church was usable for worship and the remainder of the building was left as a derelict and roofless ruin. In 1811, there was some reconstruction work done, but the church was not fully restored until the remarkable conservation programme by the Lamp of Lothian Trust in the early 1970s.

The Collegiate Church of St Mary the Virgin.

# 41. Hailes Castle

For their outing, members of the Berwickshire Naturalists' Club spent the day visiting Hailes Castle. Over 150 were present and weather conditions were pleasant. The fields of corn, some of which had been already cut, added their own note of colour to the scenery. Meeting at East Linton, cars proceeded to the road-end, which leads to Hailes Castle. Those present then proceeded on foot to the castle, which lies just at the foot of Traprain Law. Situated on a quiet, sequestered spot on the banks of the River Tyne, the castle is now in ruins, though up to the end of the eighteenth century part of it was still roofed in and used as a granary. Miss Simpson, Assistant Inspector of Ancient Monuments for Scotland, said she was very glad to welcome the Club to Hailes. Miss Simpson pointed out that the original castle would not have been of stone, for stone castles did not exist in Scotland during the twelfth century. The original castle would have been of a mote and bailey type with a wooden tower. The thirteenth century castle was built by an Earl of Dunbar and March, and additions were made in the fourteenth century by the Hepburn family, who owned it for 200 years, and who took part in some of the most stirring times in history. It was known that building operations must have been in progress at Hailes in 1507, because James VI visited the castle in that year, and there was a record of him ordering silver coins to be paid to the masons. Hailes must have been a fine place in the middle of the sixteenth century; when Lord Gray of Wilton, Governor of Berwick Castle, described the castle as a place of great beauty and strength such as was seldom seen out of England. Miss Simpson mentioned that visits had been made to Hailes by Mary Queen of Scots and by Cromwell. During the seventeenth century, Hailes was in the hands of the

*Above*: Hailes Castle.

*Below*: Hailes Castle from the river.

Setons, who sold it to Sir David Dalrymple. Pictures in old books showed that in the middle of the eighteenth century the tower was still completely roofed, and this part was used as a granary until 1835. Miss Simpson drew special attention to the stone pigeon nesting-boxes, the pit prison, the dungeon and the arrow slits in the walls. Members then visited these features and walked along outside on the river side of the castle to the old well. Returning to their cars, there was an interval for a picnic lunch in the field before the journey was resumed to Haddington.

*The Berwick Advertiser* (10 August 1939)

It sounds like an interesting and educational excursion to Hailes Castle by the members of the Berwickshire Naturalists' Club in August 1939. However, there is a degree of poignancy in the knowledge that the outbreak of the Second World War was only two weeks after the visit.

The castle grounds by the Tyne are of rare beauty. There is a miniature glen through which a tiny burn trickles to the river. Trees, grass, burn are left untouched, and so they fit well the ruined castle.

Francis Watt, *Edinburgh and The Lothians* (1912)

The substantial ruins of Hailes Castle are located around 4 miles east of Haddington along a single-track road and hidden away in a peaceful riverside setting on a bend of the River Tyne. The castle has its origins in the early thirteenth century as a fortified tower house for the Earls of Dunbar and is one of Scotland's oldest castles. It was later held by the Hepburn family and Mary, Queen of Scots was entertained by her third husband James Hepburn, 4th Earl of Bothwell, at Hailes. There are two vaulted pit-prisons and a dovecote in the original tower.

In 1686, the Dalrymples, the then owners, built a new Palladian-style country house at New Hailes, near Musselburgh, and abandoned the castle. By the nineteenth century, it was being used as a granary and subsequently fell into decay. The castle has been in state care since 1926.

# 42. Lennoxlove

Lennoxlove House is located just to the south of Haddington. It is approached by a half-mile drive fringed with oak trees. It is 'one of Scotland's most ancient and notable houses'. The Lethington estate was acquired in 1385 by the Maitland family who built an L-plan tower house. Numerous additions and alterations were carried out over the centuries to create the present mansion.

In 1703, the name was changed from Lethington to Lennoxlove. There are a number of versions of the reason for the change of name. All relate to love stories and the rich and beautiful Frances Teresa Stewart, Duchess of Lennox who was the model

*Above*: Lennoxlove.

*Right*: Lennoxlove, sundial.

for Britannia on British coins. The extensive designed landscape around Lennoxlove was originally laid out in the mid-sixteenth century. One of the highlights is the seventeenth-century sundial in the shape of an elegant lady with a sundial balanced on her head.

# 43. Gosford

Gosford House is one of the most handsome and ornate of the modern residences of Scotland. It was built by the grandfather of the present Earl of Wemyss. Situated amidst extensive and richly wooded grounds, enclosed by high stone walls, it has an outlook on the Firth of Forth. A feature of the arrangement of the grounds is a series of ponds, in which interesting collections of water fowl from many countries have been acclimatised. The house contains a valuable collection of pictures and statuary. The original house was built from designs of the brothers Adam and was completed in 1802. Extensive alterations and additions were carried through by the late Lord Wemyss, who succeeded in 1883. The mansion house has a pedimented west front, surmounted by a dome and ornamented with statuary, vases, and carving.

*Scotsman* (7 June 1928)

The beautiful pleasure grounds surrounding Gosford House were commissioned in 1790 by Francis Charteris, 7th Earl of Wemyss (1723–1808), and were designed by

Gosford, view over lake to boathouse.

*Above*: Gosford House.

*Below*: Gosford Mausoleum.

James Ramsay in a natural style. There is much to enjoy in the Gosford policies: three curving lakes, an ornamental icehouse, a shell-covered curling house and a fine boathouse all set amid parkland trees and linked by well laid out footpaths. The lakes would have been used for boating, fishing parties, curling and skating. They are now home to a range of bird life.

The neoclassical pyramid-capped mausoleum in the grounds was built around 1795 for Francis Charteris. It has space for sixty-four coffins, but the earl is the only person interred in the building. The earl was Grand Master Mason of Scotland and the pyramid is liberally adorned with Freemason symbolism.

Gosford House was designed by Robert Adam in 1790 for the Earl of Wemyss. Problems with the construction resulted in its partial demolition. It was not fully occupied until the 1890s after an extensive remodelling, including the addition of elaborate baroque pavilions, by the architect William Young in 1891. Between the wars, the house was used as a hotel. The house was occupied by the military during the Second World War, when the main rooms of the central block were badly damaged by fire. The house replaced an earlier Old Gosford House, which was demolished around 1939.

# 44. Gifford

The picturesque village of Gifford lies approximately 3 miles south of Haddington. Gifford has always been closely associated with the Yester estate. The village of Bothans in the parish of Yester, named for Saint Bothan (the patron saint of ignorance or illiteracy), had developed close to Yester Castle and, in the seventeenth century, the villagers were moved to a new planned town in the present location on the opposite side of the Gifford Water to improve the privacy of Yester House.

> In the castle of Hugh Clifford de Yester there was a capacious cavern formed by magical art, and called in the country, Bo-Hall or Hobgoblin Hall. A stair of twenty-four steps led down to this apartment, which is a large and spacious hall, with an arched roof; and though it hath stood for so many centuries, and been exposed to the internal air for a period of fifty or sixty years, it is still as firm and entire as if it had only stood a few years. From the floor of this hall, another stair of thirty-six steps leads down to a pit which hath a communication with Hopes-water.
>
> *Notes to Marmion* (1823)

Yester Castle was built in 1267 for Sir Hugo Gifford. Sir Hugo was reputed to be a wizard and was said to have constructed a large underground dungeon, known as the Goblin Hall, at the castle with the aid of supernatural forces. By the early 1700s, the Gifford family had Yester Castle demolished and moved into Yester House.

Gifford, Station Road.

Yester House.

# 45. Preston Mill

Preston Mill is possibly the most picturesque building in the Lothians. The outstanding feature of the group of buildings is the quirky polygonal kiln building with its pantiled conical roof topped by a ventilator cowl.

Grain was milled on this site for centuries and the present building dates from the eighteenth century. There were over twenty mills along the length of the Tyne at one time, processing grain from local farms and reflecting East Lothian's rich agricultural output. The proximity of Edinburgh, with its steam-powered mills, resulted in the closure of most East Lothian mills in the nineteenth century. Preston Mill continued to operate commercially producing oatmeal until 1959. The idiosyncrasy of its design may have contributed to some extent to its survival.

The mill building is a fairly plain rectangular building, which is linked by an overhead wooden foot bridge to the kiln. Grain was dried in the kiln before passing down a chute into the mill. The six-spoke mill wheel, which dates from 1909, is driven by a lade and powers all the machinery in the mill

Preston Mill.

A plaque on the west wall of the mill notes that the mill was presented to the National Trust for Scotland in January 1950 by the trustees of the late John R. Gray. The mill was renovated by the National Trust for Scotland, with help from Rank Hovis McDougall, and is maintained in working order. The adjoining two-storey cottage and stable accommodate an exhibition and shop.

# 46. Traprain Law

A remarkable find of Roman silver ware has just taken place on the summit of Traprain Law, a notable hill fortress of great antiquity on Mr. Balfour's estate of Whittingehame in East Lothian. The summit of this extraordinary mass of Trap rock has for some time been in course of excavation. Lines of fortifications, paved flooring, and other signs of ancient habitations have been discovered beneath the turf which covers the native rock. Fragments of unglazed Roman pottery, decorated Samian ware, bronze urns, and portions of glass bracelets, iron knives and shears, sharpening stones, and a cleverly devised folding spoon of bronze have all been discovered on this remarkable site, but no single discovery has equalled that which has just been made during the past month. From the top of the hill three bucket loads of Roman silver have been dis covered. Though hacked and broken, it is still covered with designs, classical in style, and beautiful in technique. It is held to be late Roman in date and in part Christian in design, the motifs including the birth of Venus, Pan, Adam and Eve, the Adoration of the Magi, and other subjects, some pagan and some Christian. One or two coins found with the silver, and one or two Teutonic pieces a silver brooch and the like suggest that Angles, Saxons, or other Germanic men looted the silver somewhere and, coming to Britain, buried it on Traprain Law, apparently in some haste. No such find has ever been made in Britain, and hardly any even on the Continent. The site, which, as we have said, has long been famous to antiquaries, is known to tradition as the home of King Loth, from which the geographic name of the Lothians is derived.

*The Sphere* (21 June 1919)

The prominent elevated oval-shaped ridge of Traprain Law is a natural landmark 4 miles east of Haddington. Historically it was known as Dunpendylaw, and the name Traprain dates from the eighteenth century. It was a prehistoric fortress and a major stronghold of the tribe known as the Votadini in the first century AD. The Votadini were later established at Din Eidyn – the castle rock of Edinburgh. A large treasure trove of Roman silver was found on the hill in 1919.

Legend has it that the 2.4-metre-high standing stone, known as the Loth Stone, close to Traprain Law, marked the grave of the Pictish King Loth from whom Lothian takes its name. The stone has been moved slightly from its original position to allow easier ploughing.

*Above*: Traprain Law.

*Left*: The Loth Stone.

# A GREAT HAUL OF SILVER in East Lothian.

The Hill of King Loth. (*The Sphere*, 21 June 1919)

# 47. Athelstaneford

Athelstaneford, pronounced locally as 'Elshinthurd', lies some 3 miles north east of Haddington. It was established by a local landowner as a planned village in the mid-eighteenth century. Low, whitewashed and red-pantiled single-storey cottages stretch along both sides of the wide road. The village is the legendary home of the Scottish Saltire. The story has it that in AD 832 a Pictish army was mustered in the area for a battle with the invading Angles. Before the battle St Andrew appeared in a vision to Óengus II, the leader of the Picts, and predicted their victory. The following day a white cross formed by clouds appeared in a blue sky and the Picts went on to win the battle. The village is also said to take its name from Athelstane, the leader of the Angles, who was killed at a local river crossing by Angus McFergus, the Pict. The legend has made Athelstaneford an important site on the Saltire Trail with the National Flag Heritage Centre based in a lectern doocot, which dates from 1583, in the village.

Doocots (dovecotes) are prominent features in the rural landscape of many parts of Lothian, as estates were relatively small and consisted of rich arable land producing fine agricultural crops, which provided an excellent source of food for the pigeons.

Pigeons provided a valuable source of year-round fresh meat and eggs, adding variety to meals in the winter months. Their droppings, which built up in the doocots, made an excellent fertiliser, and were used in the production of gunpowder and leather tanning and cloth dyeing. There was also a prevalent belief that pigeons had medicinal properties and they were used in various forms as a cure-all for everything from the plague to baldness.

There have been laws concerning doocots since 1424, when an Act relating to destroyers of dow-houses was passed. However, pigeons could have a significant

Athelstaneford Doocot.

impact on surrounding crops, and, by 1617, another statute was necessary on account of 'the frequent building of doucottis by all manner of persounes in all the parts' of the realm. This restricted the privilege of building doocots to owners of land which produced ten chalders or 160 bolls (1.25 cwt) of grain within 2 miles of the site of the doocot, in order to encourage the pigeons to feed on the landowners' crops rather than their neighbours.

Scottish doocots are of two main types. The first purpose-built doocots, dating from the sixteenth century, are beehive shaped, circular in section and tapering towards the top with a flat domed roof. The other early style is the rectangular lectern type, such as that at Athelstaneford. These have a distinctive sloping mono-pitched roof often with crow-stepped gables that provided a perch for the pigeons.

The need for doocots gradually died out at the start of the nineteenth century, as their function in providing an extra source of fresh food in wintertime became obsolete with the introduction of new farming methods that allowed for the feeding of cattle in the winter. The pigeon's habit of indiscriminate feeding was also seen as a source of social injustice (one of the minor causes of the French Revolution is said to have been the destruction of peasants' crops by pigeons owned by the French aristocracy).

Doocots are great survivors and are often the residual reminder of great estates. This is possibly due to fact that they were often converted to other uses during the nineteenth century. Another possible reason for their survival may be associated with the old superstition that the demolition of a doocot would result in a death within the year in the family of the person responsible for its removal.

# 48. Tantallon

The Queen at Tantallon. *Ding doon Tantallon; mak' a brig to the Bass* (Old Proverb). Tantallon, in its earlier days, held both sea and land at defiance. It frowned across the narrow streak of water to the Bass Rock, whose twin brother it might have been. Her Majesty during the visit with which she has just honoured the Duke and Duchess of Roxburghe was present on Monday at what is described as 'a tea party' in Tantallon Castle. A grim place for such a simple repast! The Queen's visit to the old stronghold of the Black Douglas was like the benignant light of a better time visiting the darkness of the past. How seldom has peace and gladness lighted up the dreary courts of Tantallon.

*The Aberdeen Journal* (31 August 1878)

The substantial remains of Tantallon Castle stand on the brink of a high cliff-side promontory facing the Bass Rock. With its massive curtain wall, colourful history and dramatic location, it is one of the most imposing and impressive castles in Scotland.

Tantallon Castle was built on the site of an earlier fortification by William Douglas, 1st Earl of Douglas, in the mid-fourteenth century. It was a stronghold of the Douglas family for centuries. Conflict between the Douglases and the Stewart kings resulted in the castle being besieged in 1491 and 1528. In 1651, the castle came under attack again from Cromwell's army and, after a twelve-day siege, the castle

Tantallon Castle and the Bass Rock.

Tantallon Castle.

was 'ding doon' and abandoned. It was left to decay until the end of the nineteenth century, when work was carried out to stabilise the ruins.

> And, sudden, close before them show'd
> His towers, Tantallon vast;
> Broad, massive, high, and stretching far,
> And held impregnable in war.
> On a projecting rock they rose,
> And round three sides the ocean flows,
> The fourth did battled walls enclose.
>
>         Sir Walter Scott, *Marmion* (1808)

Sir Walter Scott provides an accurate description of the castle in his narrative poem, *Marmion*. The sea and the 30-metre-high cliffs provide a natural defence on three sides of the castle, with the landward side enclosed by a massive red sandstone curtain wall. The remains of two towers project above the curtain wall at each end. The prominent middle tower houses the entrance gate.

# 49. Dirleton

Dirleton used to boast within the small orbit of its earlier world that it was the prettiest village in Scotland. This is not, to be sure, a flight to any great aesthetic heights, but Dirleton, which has not altered a bit, is assuredly a delectable little place. It mostly fronts upon a village green, one side of which is occupied by a hoary fortress of historic fame, beautifully embowered among foliage and gardens kept up with assiduous care for this last half-century. The village dwellings, each in their own gardens, though a trifle formal, look what they are, the creation of a former landlord's pride and care. An admirable old inn, where the little local golf club used in old days to sup once a year, and sup formidably as regards accessories, has the place of honour. The kirk, dignified but unbeautiful, stands retired from the green amid stately timber. Such is Dirleton. But its castle is, of course, the overwhelming attraction, and a favourite resort of golf-widows and orphans, and other visitors from North Berwick.

A. G. Bradley, *The Gateway of Scotland* (1912)

Dirleton, with its attractive stone buildings grouped around a triangular green, is one of the most picturesque villages in East Lothian. Much of its present appearance is due to the early nineteenth century 'beautification' plans of Lady Elgin (1778–1855), which transformed the agricultural village.

Dirleton from the castle.

Dirleton Castle.

The village is dominated by the striking remains of Dirleton Castle, which stand on a rocky outcrop on the east side of the village green. The castle has its origins in an early twelfth-century timber castle for the 1st Baron de Vaux, which was rebuilt in stone in the thirteenth century. In 1298, the castle was besieged by Edward I's troops during the Wars of Scottish Independence and retaken by Robert the Bruce's forces in 1311, when sections of the battlements were removed to prevent any future use of it by the English. In the fourteenth century the estate passed, by marriage, to the Halyburton family and the castle was restored and enlarged. It was attacked and taken by the Cromwell's army in 1650.

In 1663, John Nisbet, the then owner, decamped from the castle to a new mansion at Archerfield House. The castle fell into a state of ruin until it was taken into State care in the 1920s.

The splendid gardens, which include a seventeenth-century bowling green, a walled garden and a beehive dovecot, form a striking setting to the castle

# 50. Yellowcraig

The stunning 64-kilometre-long (40 miles) coastline of East Lothian is studded with wide expanses of outstanding beaches, which regularly win awards for their high standards. The beach at Yellowcraig, between Dirleton and North Berwick, is

Fidra from Yellowcraig.

one of the broadest and longest. Yellowcraig forms part of the John Muir Way, a long-distance footpath that runs from Dunbar to Helensburgh and is named for John Muir (1838–1914). Muir was born in Dunbar and after moving to the United States was instrumental in founding the country's national parks.

The day looks promising enough for an expedition to Fidra, the island with the lighthouse you can see lying up the Firth and serving as a lighthouse station under the jurisdiction of the Commissioners of Northern Lights.

The wind is against us for Fidra and by a series of zigzags we arrive at Fidra. We run into a natural harbour, which Father Ocean, assisted by Father Time, has cut out in the rocks. The lighthouse men have been on the outlook for us, and in a few moments, after a climb up the iron ladder, we stand on this island home. A steep ascent leads us to the light. Half way up the ascent are the ruins of a building representing all that remains of an old lazar-house, wherein the lepers of old once where bidden to live and die.

We are standing under the shadow of a solid brick house, from the eastern side of which the lighthouse tower springs. Here dwell the two lighthouse-keepers, the chief and his assistant. The former has wife and bairns all securely and comfortably housed in a commodious domicile. The latter is a junior and unmarried.

A climb up an iron ladder and an ascent through a trap-door bring us to the first flat of the building. Here are kept spare glasses and other stores. Then another climb and we reach the clock-work flat. The apparatus is wound every hour, and the big weight descends through the floor to the flat below as the clock runs out. Another flight upwards and we are inside the lamp. There are six lamps, which burn paraffin oil. Each lamp is set in a reflector which gleams like silver. The lights show once in 15 seconds as they rotate, and differ in this way from the Isle of May light beyond, which is a 'flasher'. Everything here goes by routine as rigid and exact as are the movements of the clock's work below. Life of this kind may be monotonous, but it clearly possesses its own advantages. Four hours on and four hours off night by night, to be whistled out of bed for duty in the winter's chill, may not be a highly inviting prospect. But there is fresh air, a healthy existence, and a freedom from many a care and worry besetting dwellers on mainlands, which must be set off against seclusion from civilization and crowds.

The lighthouse folks wave us a kindly parting. The big brown sail is hoisted, the boat scuds merrily before the wind, the outlines of Fidra become dull and dim as we speed homewards, and the rock resumes its old familiar aspect.

*The Daily News* (24 September 1886)

Yellowcraig also offers fine views of the offshore island of Fidra, which is said to have been the inspiration for the outline of the plan of the island in Robert Louis Stevenson's *Treasure Island*. The island is a RSPB reserve and the lighthouse, which was automated in 1970, dates from 1885.